JOURNEY *through* SOUTH AFRICA

JOURNEY *through* SOUTH AFRICA

Gerald Cubitt & Peter Joyce

STRUIK

Struik Publishers (Pty) Ltd
(a member of The Struik Publishing Group (Pty) Ltd
80 McKenzie Street
Cape Town 8001

Reg. No.: 54/00965/07

First published 1986
Second edition 1989
Third edition 1990
Fourth edition 1992
Fifth edition 1995

ISBN 1 86825 692 8

THE LAND AND ITS PEOPLE

South Africa is a big country; five times the size of Britain, about as large as Holland, Belgium, Italy, France and West Germany put together. It stretches from the Limpopo River in the north to blustery Cape Agulhas, nearly 2 000 kilometres to the south, from Namaqualand along the barren western seaboard 1 500 kilometres to subtropical KwaZulu-Natal and the humid Indian Ocean coast: a total land area of just under 1,3 million square kilometres.

Enclosed within South Africa are the separate kingdoms of Lesotho and Swaziland.

Far up the Atlantic coastline, beyond the desolate reaches of the Orange River, is Namibia (formerly South West Africa), a vast and beautiful country of diamonds, desert and human division that the League of Nations mandated to South Africa after the First World War and which finally gained its independence in 1990. Flanking the Republic's far northern regions are, in clockwise order, the independent black states of Botswana, Zimbabwe and Mozambique. A rich territorial diversity.

Indeed, diversity is probably the single word that best illustrates both South and southern Africa. The canvas is kaleidoscopic; variety, contrast and sometimes conflict are vividly evident in the bewildering mix of race and language, creed, colour and culture. The diversity is there, too, in the nature of the land, in its geological formations and regional climates; its mountains, plains and coasts; its rich farmlands, its bushveld scrub and deserts, each of the many different parts supporting its own distinctive plant and animal life. Truly, a world in one country.

PLATEAU AND PLAIN

In physical terms a significant portion of the land is very old. The subcontinent comprises 22 physiographic regions – different geological areas. Some of the rock strata in the valley of the Limpopo and in the northern Transvaal were formed 4 000 million years ago; not all that long, on the geological calendar, after planet earth itself began to cool. Others, those belonging to the Kalahari group, are a mere two million years old. In between is a score of classifications that, together, tell a large part of the earth's story.

This variety accounts for South Africa's broad-based wealth of mineral resources. The ancient Swazian and Rondian formations, for instance, include gold-bearing reefs that, since their discovery just a hundred years ago, have transformed the Witwatersrand's quietly rural Highveld into a giant conurbation, recognized for the past half century and more as one of the world's mining and financial capitals. More recently gold, extensive reserves of it, was located in the Orange Free State. Also in the north-central regions, but farther to the west, there are rich iron and manganese deposits. Platinum and chrome are found in the North West Province; coal in the Karoo Sequence; diamonds in the Kimberlite pipes of the Northern Cape; copper, zinc, uranium, cobalt, nickel – the list, 59 commodoties in total, extends through almost the entire spectrum of metals and minerals. The only major ingredient that has been lacking is oil, and even then significant reserves have been charted and are being exploited (albeit on a heavily subsidized basis) off the southern shores.

The lie of the land. If you were to look down on South Africa from an orbiting satellite you would see a clear, quite simple topographical pattern. The land falls into two distinct physical regions: the greater interior plateau, semicircular and occupying most of the subcontinent; and the 'marginal zone' which is the relatively narrow coastal and hinterland strip fringing the plateau on three sides. A third, strikingly obvious geographical feature is the division between the two regions: the highly (in the most literal sense) conspicuous and continuous necklace of mountains and hills known as the Great Escarpment.

The plateau is actually the southern tip of the Great African Plateau that rises in the Sahara Desert, some 5 000 kilometres to the north. In southern Africa its altitude varies from the comparatively low 600 metres of the Kalahari basin to an impressive 3 400 metres in the mountains of Lesotho.

Its subdivisions comprise, first, the basins: the bushveld north of the Transvaal uplands and the Bushmanland, and the upper Karoo – the lowest and driest parts of the plateau and known collectively as the 'middleveld'. Second, the plateau proper: vast, gently undulating plains studded with scatters of rocky outcrops and ridges (the classic Highveld, which Pretoria graces and over which Johannesburg and its urban satellites sprawl) and, in four of its subdivisions, rising to the upland 'blocks' of the Lesotho plateau to the east (the highest); the western heights that look over the southern Kalahari, and the northern ranges: the Waterberg and the Soutpansberg that roll down towards the Limpopo River.

The plateau's rim, the Great Escarpment, begins in the north-east with the craggy Transvaal Drakensberg (highest peak Mount Anderson 2 316 metres), then runs southwards, rising in even more splendid grandeur to the famed Natal Drakensberg's towering faces, some dropping near-vertically 2 000 metres to the plains below. Here are Mont-Aux-Sources (3 282 metres); Champagne Castle (3 376 metres); Giant's Castle (3 314 metres); charming and evocative names for some of the most awesome peaks in the southern hemisphere. So formidable is the range that one 250 kilometre stretch may be traversed by just a single, steep route – the Sani Pass.

Southward still, the escarpment loops inland in a series of smaller ranges: the Stormberg of Anglo-Boer War fame; the Suurberg; the Sneeuberg north of the gracious little Eastern Cape town of Graaff-Reinet. It then disappears into flatland for a while – through this thrust the major surface communications routes between Cape Town and the north – then rises in the impressive granite formations of the Roggeveld Scarp and the Kamiesberg range (1 707 metres) and into Namaqualand.

Three hundred million years ago, when the single great land mass called Pangaea first began to succumb to continental drift, slowly, over hundreds of millennia, breaking up to create the global land patterns we know today, the stretch and pull of the earth's crust fashioned the most striking portion of South Africa's marginal zone

– the Cape Fold Mountains. Legacies of the same mountain-building process are sister ranges in the Argentine and in Antarctica.

The series of Cape mountains, running parallel to each other and rising starkly over wide longitudinal valleys, includes the Olifants River, Drakenstein, Hottentots Holland and the splendid Cederberg (highest point: the 2 077 metre Greater Winterhoek north of Tulbagh) ranges in the western parts, and the more intensively folded hills of Langeberg, Outeniqua, Tsitsikamma and Swartberg in the east, an area that also contains the Little Karoo basin, 30 by 60 kilometres in extent.

A much larger basin, the wide, shallow, world-famed Great Karoo, extends from the folded belts of the south and west northwards. Generally flattish but spliced by dramatic gorges, the most spectacular of which is probably the aptly named Valley of Desolation, it is an arid region: 'karoo' is derived from the Hottentot word meaning dry or bare. But still, there is the occasional small farming village, scattered flocks of sheep and lonely homesteads in this big, strangely beautiful land.

Water in a dry land. Only a small part of South Africa is blessed by good and regular rains (see page 7). Just a quarter of the country is nurtured by perennial rivers – they flow through the southern seaboard and the eastern segment of the plateau. There are no real lakes – the large expanse of water called Fundudzi, in the Northern Transvaal, was born of a massive landslide; the tourist-frequented 'lakes' of Zululand, and the Knysna district of the southern Cape are in reality lagoons. So even the flow of the perennial streams and rivers depends on seasonal and, latterly, erratic rains. As for the great spaces of the western interior, their riverbeds fill and flow only after the rare summer rainstorms. In South Africa, water is a precious commodity.

Biggest of the river systems is that of the Orange, running westwards from its headwaters in the high Natal Drakensberg for 2 250 kilometres to the Atlantic, plunging magnificently into the granite Augrabies gorge close to the Namibian border (in exceptional seasons the flow is greater than that of the better known Victoria Falls on the Zambezi River far to the north) before embarking on its last, desolate leg to the sea. Its tributaries include the Caledon and the Vaal, which is actually longer than its big brother but less voluminous.

The Orange drains almost the entire plateau – 47 per cent of the country. The eastern slopes of the plateau, on the other hand, are comparatively well-watered by their small rivers (one of the more substantial is the Letaba, well-known to game-viewers in the Kruger National Park). They drain just 12 per cent of the country's surface area but contribute 40 per cent of the run-off. Of the other rivers of the plateau, Kiplings' 'great grey-green, greasy Limpopo' is the most renowned, demarcating South Africa's northern frontiers with Botswana and Zimbabwe, gathering volume and momentum as it makes its way eastwards to the Indian Ocean north of the Mozambique capital of Maputo. Despite its legend in literature, however, it is not a major river by African standards.

Significant rivers of the marginal zone include the Sundays and Great Fish, both of which were crucial lines in the often violent territorial disputes between white settler and black tribesman in the nineteenth century (see page 24); the beautiful Berg River of the western Cape; and Natal's Tugela, where some of the most savage and, for the British, unrewarding battles of the Anglo-Boer War were fought.

All told, though, South Africa's rivers do not amount to very much in world terms. Put together, their total run-off is equivalent to that of the Rhine at Rotterdam, and to just half that of the mighty Zambezi 1 000 kilometres to the north and about the same as the Mississippi in the United States.

Supplementary to the river systems are hundreds of pans, or 'floors' – shallow stretches of sometimes salty water (the result of evaporation), biggest of which is the 40 by 64 kilometre Groot Vloer in the north-western Cape. But the country's resources remain limited and precious; much of the modest volume is lost through spillage and through evaporation in the intense heat, and there is an ever-increasing demand from the farms, the cities and from industry. Consequently a number of ambitious hydro-engineering projects have been launched, some completed. Among them is the Orange River Scheme, which accumulates an annual 7 500 million m³ of water, irrigates 300 000 hectares of farmland and provides an extra 2 200 million m³ for urban use. Its infrastructure includes the huge Hendrik Verwoerd and P.K. le Roux dams and a system of underground waterways, one of which is 82,5 kilometres long – the largest continuous water tunnel in the world. It irrigates the Great Fish River Valley.

Even grander in concept and scale is the Lesotho Highlands Water Scheme, one of the most ambitious civil engineering exercises ever undertaken in the southern hemisphere. It is designed eventually (in the second decade of the 21st century) to supply the PWV area and its environs with a massive 63,6 million m³/sec rate of water, effectively doubling the annual flow into the Vaal basin, and at the same time to supply all of Lesotho's electrical power needs. The first of the three phases will, when completed in the later 1990s, produce about 17 million m³/secs of water. The scheme involves the creation of an extensive road network over some of the continent's most rugged terrain, hundreds of kilometres of tunnelling, and a number of the world's largest rock-fill dams.

Vegetation. With the settlement of South Africa by black people from the north and by white colonists who created an enclave at the Cape in the 1650s and then spread steadily eastwards and northwards (see Part II, *The Past*), much of the land was denuded of its natural vegetation, the cover either destroyed or replaced by exotic species. Nevertheless, five major groups, or vegetation communities, are clearly distinguished. They are those of:

■ *The deserts and semi-deserts.* Excluding the huge and desolate expanses of the Namib, which are not within the Republic's borders, two areas fall into these categories. South Africa's only true desert region lies along the westward strip of Namaqualand extending into the lower Orange River Valley, a parched region that averages – depending on the precise locality – a scant 50 to 150 millimetres of rainfall a year. In some years there is no rainfall at all. Vegetation is appropriately meagre: a thin ground cover of low, hardy, widely spaced shrubs and succulents and, in springtime, a blaze of bright desert annuals. One notch higher on the vegetation scale is the Great Karoo, an enormous area of semi-desert with an uncertain rainfall averaging between 125 and 375 millimetres a year. Again, plant life comprises sparse, tough shrubs and succulents, though grasses occur – and sustain sheep where the veld is properly managed – in the more tolerable eastern regions.
■ *The Mediterranean* (winter rainfall) areas of the south-western and southern Cape. Because of the immense wealth of its plant life, and despite its tiny area, this botanical region is regarded as one of the six floral kingdoms of the world. Forests are to be found only in the wetter kloofs, but many evergreen shrubs of various heights occur in this region as well as a vast number of indigenous species known collectively as *fynbos*. This includes the Cape's famed proteas (the king protea is South Africa's national flower), ericas and a marvellous diversity of bulbs.
■ *The bushveld* covering the lower slopes of the plateau and the Lowveld of the eastern Transvaal, an area that encompasses the great expanse of the Kruger National Park. Flora in the northern

parts includes marula and umbrella thorn, the elephantine baobab, the fever tree, the ubiquitous dark-green mopani and tall tufted grasses. In the more open Kalahari thornbush country, mainly towards the west, there are hardy acacia and camel-thorn trees and sparse semi-desert ground cover.

■ *The temperate interior uplands*. This is the classical veld consisting of rolling grassy plains and, probably because of winter droughts and frost, few trees – although some exotic species such as willows and eucalyptus (gum trees) thrive.

■ *The scattered forests* of the year-round rainfall belt, once widespread but victim to the depredations of man over the centuries. The relicts of the marginal zone's great woodlands are now protected by law. Most extensive is the strip, 180 by 16 kilometres, along the southern coast where tall ironwood, yellowwood and stinkwood trees occur. Farther to the north, along the Natal coast, there are patches of evergreen subtropical tree species, including palms and, in the swampier areas, mangroves.

SEAS AND SHORES

Lapped by two oceans, South Africa's coastline runs 3 000 kilometres from the Atlantic wilderness of the Orange River mouth in the north-west, round the Cape to northern KwaZulu-Natal and the Mozambique border in the east. Large stretches reward the traveller with spectacular scenery; some are a paradise for the angler, the surfer, the camper and the sun-worshipper.

Broadly speaking, the oceans fall into two type-categories: warm and cooler, the nature of each determined largely by the dominant currents. The warm waters on the east coast of South Africa emanate from the tropics and flow rapidly south and south-west as the Agulhas Current, which more or less hugs the coast until, near Cape Aghulhas, it turns south and east.

Along the west coast, the main waterbody comes from the South Atlantic as the north-flowing Benguela Current, and is much cooler. West of Cape Point and to the north, wind characteristics play a major role in determining water temperatures – strong offshore winds of the summer months cause coastal upwelling of cold water (as low as 7 °C) from the subsurface north-flowing Benguela Current; onshore or light winds reverse this process and are dominant in winter, when the average temperature is about 14,5 °C. Thus, because of the configuration of the coast in the vicinity of the Cape Peninsula and of the prevailing wind patterns, the summer water temperatures between False Bay, open only on its south side, and Table Bay can differ by as much as 10 °C or 12 °C. Indeed, the Cape Peninsula is full of contrasts: apart from the 'two-oceans' syndrome, the monolithic presence of Table Mountain has a profound effect upon local weather conditions: the suburb of Newlands has a much higher rainfall than Sea Point; Clifton's sea can be glass-calm while a force four gale blusters over the waters off Milnerton.

The west coast is a strange, barren region of rocky, sand-blown shorelines backed by raised beaches and, stretching inland for anything between 30 and 50 kilometres, terraces of deep, soft, often-shifting sand. Dunes are covered by sparse greenery (technically, dwarf bush vegetation), and the land is classed as 'sandveld'. In the far north, around the mouth of the Orange, the legendary raised beaches are rich with diamonds, swept down by the river over the ages and then distributed by inshore currents.

The country's dynamic fishing industry has its home along the length of the west coast. Here, during the upwelling of the Atlantic – usually in spring and summer – rich plant nutrients are carried to the inshore zone, thus favouring the proliferation of plankton, basic to the area's rich stocks of mussels. These shellfish are primary feeders, and in their turn they support massive populations of rock

lobsters, snoek and stockfish (Cape hake); in the south the sea at times abounds with tunny, marlin and yellowtail.

The south and east coasts are much more heavily populated and, in tourist terms, more popular. In the south, one stretch of shoreline with its hinterland is especially beautiful: the 220-kilometre Garden Route that extends roughly from Mossel Bay in the west to the Tsitsikamma Forest and Storms River in the east. This is a green and flowered region of charming bays and beaches, cliffs and pounding surf overlooked by the not-too-distant and quite splendid Outeniqua Mountains.

Equally enticing to holiday-makers are the coasts north and south of Durban in the east: wide, dune-backed sandy strips fringing a remarkably straight shoreline (Durban itself, with its 16 kilometre-long Bluff, is something of an exception).

In fact, there are precious few good natural harbours along the entire length of the Republic's coastline. (Saldanha Bay is the best, but it was passed over by the early seafarers in favour of the more exposed but better watered Table Bay.) It is an even coastline, without many pronounced embayments, and most of the otherwise-suitable estuaries are inhibited by sandbars, the product of currents and the heavy sediment brought by rivers with steep gradients and sporadic flow. East London, in the far eastern Cape, is the country's only river port and its harbour, on the Buffalo, is subject to constant dredging operations. Durban's bar is particularly notorious. The city's port is one of the hemisphere's biggest and busiest, but it was only in 1892, after decades of frustrating experiments with breakwaters and sand-pumps, that the 2 820-ton *Dunrobin Castle* managed to sail into harbour – the first ocean-going liner to do so.

CLIMATE

Weather patterns, influenced by different ocean currents, by altitude and prevailing winds and by the ever-changing nature of the land, are subject to sharp regional variation. Climatically, South Africa could be half a dozen entirely separate countries.

When it comes to rainfall, however, there are three broad but distinct regions. The south-western tip of the subcontinent, centring round the lovely city of Cape Town, has winter precipitation; the southern and eastern coastal belts enjoy (in good years) perennial showers which are heavy, almost tropical in KwaZulu-Natal. Rains over the rest of the country – on the great central plateau and towards the east – come with sudden summer thunderstorms brought by north-easterly winds.

This is not to say that the land, as a whole, is well-watered. On the contrary, South Africa is one of the world's drier countries: mean annual rainfall is little over 460 millimetres compared with a global average of 857 millimetres. The rains, too, tend to be unpredictable; drought has been the norm rather than the exception in recent times. And the farther west one goes the less generous the heavens are: along the shores of the Indian Ocean and in the KwaZulu-Natal hinterland a healthy 1 000 millimetres of rain can be expected to fall each year; in the western extremities of the country the average tends to be around 200 millimetres, and some of the thirstlands are lucky if they get 50 millimetres.

Average annual temperatures are more constant. The northern areas are not, as one might perhaps expect, very much hotter than the southern because the land rises to the high central plateau, which is generally cooler than other parts of the world lying within the same lines of latitude. Cape Town can be suffocating and its annual average temperature is 17 °C; Pretoria, a full 1 500 kilometres nearer the tropics, can freeze and its annual average is only half a degree more. But again, air temperatures in the east are generally higher than those in the western coastal regions, affected

SETTLEMENT AND CONQUEST. During the late fifteenth and in the sixteenth century Portuguese navigators, in the service of God and for the commercial profit of their royal patrons, charted the wind-blown shores of southern Africa, rounded the Cape and established sea-lanes to the spice-rich islands of the Indies. But the first permanent white settlement at the southern tip of Africa was Dutch, the seminal event the landing of Jan van Riebeeck and his small party of Dutch East India Company employees in April 1652. The Dutch ruled for 150 years before finally relinquishing control to Britain in 1806. In this time, they pushed their frontiers northwards and eastwards where they came into contact, and often bloody conflict, with the Nguni people. British solutions to

the border troubles included large-scale immigration schemes; the Boer reaction to an alien administration and to debilitating warfare against the Xhosa was to trek – to Natal and, more importantly, north across the Orange and Vaal rivers and into the domains of black chieftains, most powerful of whom was the redoubtable Mzilikazi. Meanwhile, the British were busy colonizing the eastern seaboard. By the late 1870s they had established their authority over the Zulu nation and, with the help of indentured Indian labour, were farming the lush land of Natal.

A Portuguese expedition plants a *padrão* – a stone cross – on the west coast (1). Van Riebeeck's arrival in Table Bay (2). The Bushmen (3) were the subcontinent's dominant race before being swept into near-oblivion, first by successive migrations of Bantu-speaking peoples and then by the relentless encroachments of white men. Huguenot refugees (4) joined the small Dutch community in 1688. British troops at the Cape, 1814 (5). The landing of the first British settlers in the eastern Cape 1820 (6). Lord Charles Somerset (7), architect of the Cape's 'anglicization' programme. The Voortrekkers hold off Mzilikazi's impis at the Battle of Vechtkop, 1836 (8). British and Xhosa do battle during the War of the Axe (9), the seventh of nine frontier wars fought between 1779 and 1878. The Zulu king Shaka grants land around Port Natal to Lieutenant Farewell and his small band of British traders, 1824 (10). Indentured Indian labourers landing at Durban (11).

respectively by the warm Agulhas and the cold Benguela currents. Temperature inversions also vary quite dramatically from place to place. They are least at the coast and greatest in the interior, where clear-skied winter nights are bitterly cold while the days remain sunny and mild.

South Africa, in fact, is blessed with a great deal of sunshine, the average number of cloud-free hours a day varying (depending on the area) from about 7,5 to 9,4 compared with New York's 6,9, Rome's 6,4 and London's 3,8 hours of sunshine a day. Some parts of the country, the dust-dry western districts for instance, register a bare ten or so overcast days a year.

The climate of the interior, in the rising lands beyond the Escarpment, is fairly uniform: bone-dry, sunny winters; summer days (from about November to February) of mounting storm clouds and late-afternoon downpours. At least, that is the traditional pattern in the north-central and eastern parts, where, apart from Kimberley in the Northern Cape, the inland cities and most of the towns are situated.

The climates of the different seaboard regions are more variable and interesting. The south-western part of the Western Cape – Cape Town, the Peninsula, its coastal extensions and hinterland – is unique within the southern African context in its Mediterranean character. It has dry summers with long, cloudless days which are sometimes – in what are called 'berg wind conditions' (hot air blowing in from the northern interior) – perfect in their somnolent stillness, at other times disturbed by a gusty, unnerving south-easter that often reaches gale-force and can last for up to a week or more. In winter it is wet and cool – downright cold at times (snow falls on the surrounding mountains). The best Cape months are those of its brief spring (September and October) and autumn (March and April) when colours are changing and the fragile delicacy of the air lifts and sustains the spirit.

Northwards, up the Namaqualand coastal districts, the climate becomes even drier and hotter until you eventually get to the Orange River and the endless, waterless tracts of the Namib Desert. Springtime in Namaqualand, though, is a lotion for the eyes: for a few brief weeks the barren desert countryside is transformed by multicoloured carpets of small, exquisite flowers.

Along the other coast, stretching east to Port Elizabeth, the climate changes from Mediterranean to temperate. Again the summers are warm (and windy); the winters cool. Here there is rainfall all year round – or there should be: the Eastern Cape, like most of the rest of the country, has at times suffered crippling droughts. Following the Indian Ocean coastline as it inclines northwards, one enters the subtropical region of KwaZulu-Natal, where it is hot and stickily humid in summer (though the uplands are cooler and very pleasant); chilly to warm in winter; and rainy throughout, but wetter during the summer months.

THE PEOPLE

South Africa has an estimated population of around 40 million. One cannot be more exact because although censuses are periodically taken they are soon outdated, and the very nature of society and the mobility – and until recently the hostility – of some of its elements have made it difficult, if not impossible, to paint a precise statistical picture.

Of the four major ethnic groups, black people numbered some 30 million in the early 1990s, whites nearly five million, those of Asian origin just under a million and the mixed-descent (coloured) community between three and four million.

Growth rates vary quite sharply among groups – predictably, since South Africa is anything but homogeneous. Most blacks have their roots in the countryside. They are of peasant farming stock,

their traditional communities tribally structured. Cultural taboos and perceived economic necessity inhibit family planning: the extended family is an accepted and effective form of social security. Southern Africa is no different from the rest of the world: the poorer, less educated tend to have large families. With greater urbanization and higher standards of living a decline in the birth rate can be expected. At present, the black population is increasing by 2,7 per cent a year, which projects a total of close to 40 million by the end of the century. By contrast, the annual white growth rate is 1,5 per cent, indicating (if one discounts the migration factor) a figure of about 5,5 million in the year 2000. The mixed-descent community's yearly rate of increase is two per cent; the Asian 2,4 per cent.

The richness of the land and of what lies beneath it have dictated the concentrations of population. There are relatively high densities along the southern and eastern seaboards, in the KwaZulu-Natal interior, the Pretoria-Witwatersrand-Vereeniging region, the Eastern Transvaal and in the central Orange Free State.

A crucial feature of the past few decades has been urban drift, the migration of people – especially black people – from their countryside to the cities. Industrial expansion since the Second World War has meant jobs, or at least the prospect of jobs, in and around the major centres: an irresistible lure to the hundreds of thousands who would otherwise have to scratch a meagre living from the soil in areas that are not favoured by many modern amenities, and where, because of drought and overstocking and erosion, much of the land is poor and becoming even poorer. With the dismantling of apartheid and the coincident pressures of drought and deep economic recession (both were features of the early 1990s), the rate of urbanization has increased dramatically. In 1993 it was estimated that 700 000 people were abandoning the rural life each year.

Biggest of the conurbations is the Pretoria-Witwatersrand-Vereeniging complex, now embraced by the PWV political region (see page 14), South Africa's industrial heartland. This immense cluster of concrete nuclei, each ringed by its dormitory suburbs, has a population of some eight million; it covers less than one per cent of the country's land area but is home to about a fifth of its people. Soweto – acronym for South-Western Townships – started life as a collection of 'locations' housing 'temporary' labour for Johannesburg's gold mines. It is now a city in its own right, one of around two million souls (that is the official figure; in reality it probably accommodates a great many more), and its commuters include highly qualified people – artisans, executives, professional folk – as well as miners, labourers, the self-employed and the unemployed.

Other centres – Cape Town, Port Elizabeth, Durban-Pinetown – have grown in similar fashion if rather less spectacularly. One source estimates that the 17 million urban blacks in South Africa are expected to increase to well over 60 million by the year 2050, posing 'one of the major population problems of the next century'. Certainly, mass-migration to the cities is not and cannot be trouble-free, but urban drift is now regarded not so much a problem as a natural, unstoppable process that could in fact help short-circuit, or at least alleviate, some of the country's most worrying ailments: badly needed infrastructural, social and other services, for instance, can be more easily and cheaply created for large concentrations of people than for widely scattered rural populations. Such endeavours as decentralization and influx control have proved enormously costly in terms of money, social relations and human dignity and are seen to have failed dismally. The new freedom of movement will indeed lead to the creation of huge urban communities, but it is easier to provide people with jobs, with houses and clinics and schools, electric lighting, proper sanitation and all the other ingredients of a decent life if they are close to and part of the established centres. Moreover, quite apart from their potential as reservoirs of manpower, technical skills and professional expertise, large urban concentrations have a habit of becoming economically self-generative – much to their own and everybody else's benefit. This is the way many of South Africa's decision-makers are thinking, and the trend indicates a radical and healthy departure from the assumptions of the past.

Increasingly, as political freedom opens the doors to social democracy in the new South Africa, it will become possible to write about the people without qualification along racial lines. But today's reality is that the racial groups have not shared a common heritage and are not, for reasons of history, of past regulation and in some cases of choice, fully integrated. Any objective summary must therefore take account of the separate identities.

The black people. Although there are close historical and cultural affinities, the blacks of southern Africa do have their ethnic divisions: they are distinguished by custom, social system and language into a number of groupings. The divisions are not clearly evident in the party-political arena (the African National Congress, for example, draws its support from all quarters) nor in the context of increasingly detribalized urban life, but in other respects the principal black groups can be regarded as distinctive societies. They comprise the Zulu, the Xhosa, the Swazi (all three are related, belonging to the Nguni group of people); the Northern Sotho, the Southern Sotho and the Tswana (again, of the same major Sotho groups; the Tswana are the western branch); the South Ndebele and the North Ndebele; the Venda and Lemba; and the Shangaan-Tsonga. To elaborate a little:

■ The two biggest components of the northern Nguni are the Swazi, now largely settled in the independent kingdom of Swaziland in the north-eastern part of the subcontinent (although the KaNgwane area, a former self-governing national state within South Africa, is home to hundreds of thousands of their kinsmen); and the Zulu, a name now given to the many subgroups of the Nguni people who were forged into a single, powerfully coherent society by the great nineteenth-century leader Shaka.

Zululand, a loosely defined region – it extends from the Tugela River north to the borders of Swaziland and Mozambique – is the historical home of the eastern Nguni people. They number around seven million, which makes them the largest of the country's 'ethnic blocks'. Their political leader (in all but name) is Chief Mangosuthu Buthelezi, their spiritual leader King Goodwill Zwelethini, guardian of their ancestral lands and cultural heritage. Until recently their 'homeland' was the quasi-independent national state of KwaZulu, a creation of the white government's 'grand apartheid' design. Both men held out strongly for continued Zulu autonomy during the protracted constitutional negotiations of the early 1990s – a stand that triggered tragic loss of life and, at one point, led to the brink of civil war – but both agreed to a last-minute compromise within the new federal dispensation (see page 39). Buthelezi, who fought long and hard against apartheid and for democracy, accepted the post of Home Affairs minister in the government of national unity. However, he remains under no illusions about the problems that face an over-centralized administration in an ethnically diverse state, and is in favour of a further devolution of power to the regions. The Zulu people, he believes, must be in control of their own destiny.
■ The southern Nguni comprise a number of sub-groups, most numerous being the Pondo, Tembu and, especially, the Xhosa, with whom the white settlers of the Cape came into bloody contact in the eighteenth and nineteenth centuries, waging nine full-scale frontier wars (see page 24). These Nguni have traditionally occupied the Transkei and Ciskei areas, which for a time functioned as quasi-independent republics before being reincorporated into the newly demarcated Eastern Cape province in 1994.

■ The Ndebele people in the north are related to the Matabele of Zimbabwe, who are of Nguni origin – their founder, Mzilikazi, rebelled against Shaka and, at the conclusion of a blood-soaked odyssey, led his followers north of the Limpopo in 1838. The Ndebele of the Northern Transvaal, many of whom are settled in what was, until 1994, the self-governing national state of KwaNdebele, are in turn divided into their southern and northern sections. The southern group has retained its Nguni heritage. The northern group, however, relinquished its Nguni identity and language and is now integrated into Sotho culture.

The Sotho, to confuse matters even further, also fall into three separate though related groups:

The Northern Sotho of whom the Pedi are the largest segment, inhabit the Lebowa area of the Northern Transvaal. The Southern Sotho make up the population of the former national state of Lebowa; the Southern Sotho live in the QwaQwa area of the Orange Free State province and, more significantly, populate the adjacent and independent kingdom of Lesotho. Thirdly, there are the Tswana of the once-autonomous republic of Bophuthatswana, a scatter of territories that embraced the town of Mmabatho and the glittering tourist mecca of Sun City. Other Tswana groups make up a great proportion of the population of neighbouring Botswana.
■ The vhaVenda, who number about 400 000, also had their own independent state until reincorporation in 1994. The Venda area is home, too, to the still-distinctive but increasingly assimilated Lemba people.
■ Finally, the Shangaan-Tsonga, something over a million strong, are neighbours of the vhaVenda and Northern Sotho. The Shangaan people in fact straddle the South African-Mozambique border, the South African section inhabiting the Gazankulu area of the Northern Transvaal province.

All this might suggest that South Africa's black communities have clung tenaciously to traditional African ways and remain outside the mainstream of western influence, which of course is patently not so. Custom, tradition and ancient loyalties do persist, most obviously but not exclusively in the rural areas. They are enshrined, for instance, in the rules of courtship and marriage (usually those sanctioning polygamy); in matters of inheritance and guardianship, and seniority within the clan; in kinship bonds, the social order and the spiritual force of ancestry; and in the assumptions underlying land tenure and in concepts of wealth.

That is the old Africa. The new co-exists (often uncomfortably) and will in due course supersede. Many of the millions of urban blacks are second and third generation townsmen; hundreds of thousands are migrant workers; all have been dramatically exposed to the blessings and curses of the acquisitive society. The tribal order, in the towns, has been largely eroded, to be replaced by a transitional but distinct subculture that encompasses (engulfs, in many tragic instances) everything from social structure and family life to music, literature and language.

Whether urbanization and its multiple assault on African tradition is a good or a bad thing, is a complex issue, the conclusion subjective. What is no longer open to question, though, is the inevitability of the process. South Africa is an industrial nation, governed by a new black establishment, dependent on the skills of the largely black workforce to keep the production lines moving. The poorer people for their part are impelled to go – and to live – where there is work. And so the sprawl of the cities continues, shifting the economic balance.

Black South Africans have dictated the course of the nation's affairs since 1994. And although much of the body economic is still controlled by the white business community, they command enormous muscle in the workplace, a strength they are able to demonstrate through legitimate trade union negotiation and action (and, sporadically, through the less formal means of consumer boycott). Certainly, this had profound implications during the last years of white political dominance, and will continue to exert powerful pressures on the new order.

Organized labour is a key player in the political arena, a socialist-leaning force that seeks to influence economic strategy at the highest level, and to improve the lot of the workers through both collective bargaining and political mass action. There have been few signs, however, that labour leaders fully appreciate, or are overly concerned with, the need to link wage levels with productivity. And unless mechanisms can be devised to create such a link, there will be a growing emphasis within the industrial and business sectors on capital intensive investment, leading to curtailed employment opportunities, perhaps even to a nominal shrinkage of the labour force. South Africa is already burdened with massive unemployment; less than one in ten school-leavers is able to find work in the formal economy, a situation which is having serious repercussions throughout the socio-economic spectrum. In these circumstances, efforts to find common ground between government, big business and the trade unions assume crucial significance.

The Asian people. A need for labour to harvest the crops of Natal's new and vast sugar plantations in the mid-nineteenth century prompted the importation of thousands of workers from India. They were indentured (contracted) for between three and five years, after which they had the choices of repatriation, of renewing their contracts, or of accepting Crown land and remaining as settlers. Most took up the land option.

The first shipload disembarked in 1860. In due course they were joined by non-indentured 'passenger' immigrants from the Indian subcontinent – British subjects able to travel freely within the Empire, and choosing the sunbathed spaces of Natal as their future home. Today, South Africa's Asian community numbers some 900 000, most of whom – 85 per cent – live in and around the Durban-Pinetown complex. Nearly all the remainder, about 100 000 people of Asian origin, are settled on the Witwatersrand and in Pretoria. Among them are 10 000 or so citizens of Chinese extraction who retain their own cultural identity.

The Indian society, generally a prosperous one, has its own distinct traditions, underpinned by religion and by the *kutum* – the disciplined, patriarchal extended family which regulates relationships and social interaction. The community is remarkably unified but also organized according to faith – Hindu and Muslim. The Hindu element is in turn divided into four language groups (Tamil, Telegu, Hindustani and Gujarati) and subscribes to its own fairly strict rules governing modes, manners, ritual, food and drink. The Muslims speak Gujarati – the language of western India – and Urdu, and observe precisely defined codes of belief and behaviour.

Again, though, traditions are being eroded, especially among the younger generation. The izar and qami, the dawni and sari are giving way, if not always to T-shirts and jeans, certainly to the more conservative western styles of dress; there is movement away from the multiple towards the smaller family; traditional male authority no longer goes unquestioned; young Indian women lead far freer and more diversified lives than their mothers and grandmothers; and English is by and large the means of communication.

Always a significant component of the South African economy – the community has an exceptionally high proportion of professionals and entrepreneurs – the Indians only recently attained full political rights. They were, though, the first to challenge prejudice and formal discrimination. The Natal Indian Congress was formed in 1894 by Mohandas Gandhi, the Mahatma ('Great Soul'), and, under his leadership and inspiration, conducted courageous and partially successful 'passive resistance' campaigns between 1906 and 1914. The organization gave birth to the Transvaal Indian Congress and, in 1920, to the nationwide South African Indian Congress (SAIC). The SAIC remained a moderate pressure group until the passage of the 1946 Asiatic Land Tenure Act (which, among other things, placed severe limitations on Indian ownership and occupation of land), but thereafter it became increasingly militant. In 1949 it allied itself to the African National Congress, and in 1954 formally endorsed the Freedom Charter, manifesto of the most powerful of the liberation movements.

South Africans of mixed descent. The country's three million-strong coloured community, the majority of whom live in the western Cape, has diverse origins. The early Dutch settlers imported slaves from Holland, from elsewhere in Africa and from some of the islands of the Atlantic and Indian oceans, and admixtures steadily and inevitably followed, Hottentot, Xhosa and white man adding their own progeny over the following decades.

Significant subgroups include the Griquas of the north-eastern and north-western regions, the product of European-Hottentot miscegenation; the mixed-decent people of Natal, many of whom trace their ancestry to immigrants from Mauritius and St Helena; and the 200 000 Cape Muslims of the Peninsula, a close-knit society that has maintained its strict Islamic ways over the centuries since their forebears arrived from Indonesia, Malagasy, Ceylon (now Sri Lanka) and China.

In general terms, though the coloured people of South Africa are culturally very much part of the western world. Some 87 per cent are of the Christian faith; the majority speak Afrikaans; and they are barely separable in lifestyle, social organization and aspiration from people of exclusively European origin. There seems no good reason why they should have been subject to any special classification (not that formally imposed ethnic categories of any kind can be justified), and in fact were more or less an integrated part of the Cape community as a whole until fairly recently, enjoying, among other things, the constitutionally entrenched common-roll franchise – until it was removed in the 1950s. Coloured residential areas were delineated; the famed District Six, close to the heart of Cape Town, was demolished in the late 1970s and early 1980s and most of its inhabitants moved to huge, new and somewhat characterless townships such as Mitchell's Plain on the Cape Flats. The move was not a popular one and the site of District Six remains largely undeveloped, a scar on Cape Town's landscape and on the minds of its citizens.

The coloured people now have strong representation within the Western Cape's provincial cabinet and legislature, and hold a number of key posts within the central government.

The white people. For much of the 20th century South Africa had two official languages (there are now eleven, though English is inexorably gaining favour as the principal means of communication), reflecting the dual origins of what was the country's politically dominant cultural groups.

The Afrikaners are descendants of the early Cape-Dutch settlers and of people of the other nationalities they absorbed, together numbering something over 2,5 million today. High Dutch was the stem from which the language branched, taking on new words and a different shape over three centuries of isolation from the original homeland and, later, from the principal Cape settlement.

The German and French elements are significant (and, linguistically, the black languages as well): the Afrikaners in fact have a rich mix of cultures in their blood, one official estimate pegging the ancestral ingredients at only 40 per cent Dutch; a suprising 40 per cent German; 7,5 per cent British (mainly Scots); 7,5 per cent French and five per cent others. The French connection, through the hardy Protestant Huguenots who fled Europe in the 1680s, can be discerned in names such as Du Plessis, Du Toit and Marais; the Dutch in the 'van' prefixes. Curiously, there seems to be very little that is clearly German in language, custom or nomenclature – assimilation seems to have been total.

Over the decades, the Afrikaner community expanded from very small beginnings, more as a consequence of natural increase than from immigration (hence the proliferation of certain names – Botha, Malan, Du Plessis and so on. Families have always tended to be large, patriarchal, Calvinistic and close-knit; groups of families clannish – the universal characteristics of pioneer people.

Despite the mixture of antecedents, and despite bouts of bitter factionalism, the story of the Afrikaner has been one of fierce pride in nation, of unity under threat, and of tough and uncompromising cultural exclusivity. All of which is understandable enough: the early settlers, especially those of the eastern Cape, found plenty of lonely hardship in a land made inhospitable by the elements, natural hazard and the violence of man, and came to trust for survival in musket, Bible and the closing of ranks. Then, with the establishment of British rule, at the beginning of the nineteenth century, came greater bureaucratic control, a degree of deprivation and a threat to their identity. So in the 1830s they inspanned their ox-wagons and trekked into the great northern wilderness in search of peace, living-space and the right to live their own lives unmolested, none of which they found in lasting measure. Fabulous deposits of gold were located beneath the pastoral surface of their Promised Land; foreigners flocked into the fledgling Boer states and once again the Afrikaners felt themselves besieged, a fear that was brutally confirmed by the Jameson Raid of 1895-96 and the cynical diplomatic prelude to full-scale war three years later (see Part II, *The Past*).

In short, from their early settler years, Afrikaners saw themselves as a hounded and beleaguered people – and with some justice. It was only towards the middle of the present century that Afrikanerdom – not the bridge-building kind of Louis Botha and Smuts but the Afrikanerdom of J.B.M. Hertzog, D.F. Malan and H.F. Verwoerd – could challenge English-speaking South Africans for economic and political dominance.

This, put briefly and perhaps simplistically, is the historical legacy. The heirs to it, in extremely broad terms, fall into two groups: those who have come to terms with the new order and play a full part in the forging of a united nation; and a diminishing conservative element who still think much like their forebearers did. The latter, driven by an age-old fear of the 'black tide', favour isolation within a *Volkstaat*, or Afrikaner people's republic.

South Africa is home to just under two million English-speaking whites, and their legacy is entirely different from that of the Afrikaners. The background is colonial rather than pioneer; urban-industrial rather than rural.

There were half a dozen watershed events (which are covered in more detail in Part II, *The Past*), in the history of the English-speaking settlement in South Africa.

First was the British occupation of the Cape (technically, two occupations: the first between 1795 and 1803, and the second from 1806 onwards) during the French Revolutionary and Napoleonic wars, when the landing of the redcoats ended over a century of Dutch East-India Company rule and ushered in an era of deliberate 'anglicization'. Part of this process was the second major influx; the arrival of 4 000 or so settlers at Algoa Bay in the eastern Cape in 1820. Farther east, the colonization of Natal – a more indepedently motivated exercise – gathered momentum from the 1840s with a series of privately organized immigration schemes.

The fourth, essentially two-pronged English onslaught, was the birth of South Africa's huge mining industry with the discovery of diamonds in the northern Cape (near present-day Kimberley) in 1867 and the accidental discovery (by two casual labourers) of gold on the Witwatersrand in the Transvaal in 1886.

These drew large numbers of *Uitlanders* (outlanders, or aliens) to the northern areas, most of whom were English-speaking. Much later, further large migrations occured after the Second World War and, in the post-colonial era, with the granting of independence to Britain's East African territories and Zambia, which produced a trickle of immigrants.

Recent years have witnessed the slow, convulsive demise of unilaterally independent white Rhodesia (now Zimbabwe), which prompted something of a flood.

The strongholds of the present English-speaking community were thus historically determined. It is no accident that South Africa's English universities are at Cape Town (UCT), Grahamstown (Rhodes University), in Natal (Durban and Pietermaritzburg) and Johannesburg (the University of the Witwatersrand). Other than significant English-speaking farming communities in the Eastern Cape and in the sugar and fruit-growing regions of KwaZulu-Natal, it is very largely an urban community.

Traces of the colonial psychology persisted until well after the Second World War. In affluent homes along the gracious tree-lined avenues of Constantia in the Cape and in Pietermaritzburg people would speak, in accents indistinguishable from those of upper-middle-class Surrey and Sussex, of England as 'home', toast the Queen on her birthday and eat plum pudding in the midday heat of a southern Christmas.

But these now represent very much of an anachronistic minority. Most English-speaking South Africans have long since detached themselves from their ancestral origins and identify wholly with the country, although some of their children, for a number of reasons unconnected with a sense of belonging, do tend to drift away, many of them to Britain.

Until fairly recently, too, the English-speaking section had virtual monopoly on the non-agrarian economy; the reins of commerce and industry were firmly in Anglo-Saxon and Jewish hands. This is no longer the case. Even before Afrikanerdom assumed control of central government and the bureaucracy in 1948 it was flexing its economic muscles. Today, despite rapid black empowerment, substantial segments of the private sector are run by Afrikaans-speakers.

A number of smaller ethnic and linguistic groups make up the residue of the white community. Most substantial – estimates vary widely but there are probably about 75 000 – are South Africans of Portuguese extraction, most of them former residents of Lisbon's African territories of Mozambique and Angola, though a substantial number hail from the Atlantic island of Madeira. In descending numerical order the additional groups are German (40 000); Greek (17 000); Italian (17 000); and French (7 000). Together, other nationalities total some 35 000.

A significant subgroup of English-speaking South Africans are the Jewish people, comprising about 2,5 per cent of the white population. Though relatively small in numbers, Jewish South Africans have contributed markedly to the business and industrial development of the country: personalities of the past such as Barney Barnato, Lionel Phillips, Samuel Marks and Alfred and Otto Beit played prominent parts in the early days of the diamond- and gold-fields. In the world of the arts, both performing and visual and in literature, so many Jews have distinguished themselves that it would be invidious to single out any name.

Among those Jews who have played significant rôles in politics the name Helen Suzman is today among the most highly respected. Celebrated both in South Africa and internationally as industrialists and philanthropists are the late Sir Ernest Oppenheimer and his son Harry, though this family is no longer of the Jewish faith.

WHERE THE PEOPLE LIVE: TERRITORIES AND CITIES

In 1910 the Crown colonies of Natal and the Cape of Good Hope and the former Boer republics of the Transvaal and the Orange Free State were brought together as provinces of the Union of South Africa. This territorial structure lasted until 1994, when the country was divided up into nine provincial regions in terms of the new federal arrangement. The former black 'homelands' – four independent republics and six self-governing national states – were reincorporated.

The regions, each with its own premier, parliament and civil service, enjoy a healthy degree of legislative and administrative autonomy. Briefly, the nine provinces are:

■ *Western Cape.* The oldest, most populous and economically advanced segment of the old Cape Province. The new region embraces Cape Town and the Peninsula; a beautiful hinterland of mountains and valleys rich in vineyards, orchards and pastures; approximately half (the more fertile half) of the country's western seaboard; the lovely south coast as far as Plettenberg Bay, and a fairly large expanse of the semi-arid Great Karoo. Capital: Cape Town; population: 3,6 million; majority political party: National Party; personal income per capita (1993): R4 188; average annual economic growth 1970-90: 2,0%.

■ *Eastern Cape.* A large, heavily populated and unevenly developed region that takes in the coastal city of Port Elizabeth and its surrounding 'settler country', the 'Border' area in the far east, and the former independent republics of Transkei and Ciskei. The major growth areas are Port Elizabeth-Uitenhage and East London-King William's Town-Bisho. Provisional capital: Bisho; population: 6,7 million; majority political party: African National Congress; personal income per capita (1993): R1 358; average annual economic growth 1970-90: 3,2%.

■ *Northern Cape.* The largest region in geographical terms – it covers 30% of South Africa, stretching from the Namaqualand seaboard in the west to the Kimberley diamond fields in the north-central part of the country – but the most sparsely populated and least developed. Much of the terrain is covered by the dry sands of the Karoo and, in the far north, the Kalahari. Capital: Kimberley; population: 760 000; majority political party: African National Congress (bare majority); personal income per capita (1993): R2 865; average annual economic growth 1970-90: 0,1%.

■ *KwaZulu-Natal.* The region corresponds, with minor adjustments, to the old Natal province and the KwaZulu homeland it incorporated, and it supports the largest of the regional populations: nearly nine million people are crowded into the 92 000 square kilometres that lie between the grandness of the Drakensberg and the warm waters of the Indian Ocean. Capital: Pietermaritzburg and Ulundi were vying for capital status at the time of writing; population: 8,5 million; majority political party: Inkatha Freedom Party; personal income per capita (1993): R1 910; average annual economic growth 1970-90: 3,1%.

■ *Orange Free State.* The province, on the high, bare plains of the central plateau, occupies about a tenth of South Africa's land area, yields a third of its maize and wheat harvests and sustains 80% of its sheep and a substantial percentage of cattle populations. Mining output includes gold, diamonds, platinum and coal. Capital: Bloemfontein; population: 2,8 million; majority political party: African National Congress; personal income per capita (1993): R2 419; average annual economic growth 1970-90: 5,5%.

■ *North West.* This comprises the former western Transvaal and part of the former northern Cape, and is something of a cinderella region. It has its platinum, chrome and other mines (around Rustenburg and Klerksdorp) but the economy is increasingly dependent on farming: fruit, vegetables and flowers around the beautiful Magaliesberg hills; great fields of golden maize elsewhere. The region encompasses most of the former republic of Bophuthatswana and its tourist playground of Sun City. Capital: Mmabatho; population: 3,3 million; majority political party: African National Congress; personal income per capita (1993): R1 789; average annual economic growth 1970-90: 2,0%.

■ *Northern Transvaal.* A region of bushveld, rich grasslands and enchanting hills (notably the Waterberg and, near the Limpopo River, the Soutpansberg). There are no major growth points – the Pietersburg area, its largest centre, accounts for just 0,6% of the country's employment – and the province lags far behind the field in the development stakes. Its tourism potential, though, is excellent: among other things it encompasses half the Kruger National Park. Capital: Pietersburg; population: 5,2 million; majority political party: African National Congress; personal income per capita (1993): R725; average annual economic growth 1970-90: 1,0%.

■ *Eastern Transvaal.* The second smallest region with the fastest growing economy. Industry is concentrated around the mining centres of Witbank and Middelburg on the highveld plateau to the west; in the east are the splendid mountains of the Transvaal Drakensberg and, beyond, the heat-hazed, game-rich Lowveld plain and the Kruger National Park. Capital: Nelspruit; population: 2,9 million; majority political party: African National Congress; personal income per capita (1993): R2 164; average annual economic growth 1970-90: 6,8%.

■ *PWV.* The name, an odd name for a geographical entity and likely to be changed, is an acronym for Pretoria-Witwatersrand-Vereeniging, the principal urban areas (see page 15). This is a small, rich, densely populated region: it generates nearly 40 per cent of the national product and around 370 people are crammed into each of its 19 000 square kilometres.

The PWV originally drew its wealth from the gold mines of the Witwatersrand – which gave birth to the city of Johannesburg – but now boasts a hugely diverse industrial economy (see further on). Capital: Johannesburg; population: 6,9 million; majority political party: African National Congress; personal income per capita (1993): R4 992; average annual economic growth 1970-90: 2,0%.

The main centres. Since Union in 1910 the country has enjoyed the luxury of three capital cities: to propitiate the most important of the rival regional interests the Union negotiators settled on Cape Town, Pretoria and Bloemfontein as the respective seats of the legislature, administration and judiciary. A powerful body of northern politicians, however, now wants to confer comprehensive capital status on Pretoria, a move strenuously opposed by Capetonians. The debate is likely to continue, acrimoniously, for years, and it could prove highly divisive.

South Africa's principal urban centres, in order of age, are:

■ *Cape Town,* which had its beginnings in 1652 with the landing of Jan van Riebeeck and his small party of settlers. Greater Cape Town – the magisterial districts of the Cape, Goodwood, Kuils River, Wynberg and Simon's Town – sprawls over much of the Peninsula and is home to a rapidly growing African population which will reach a million well before decade's end. Its mixed-descent (coloured) community numbers 900 000, its white population hovers around the half-million mark.

The city's setting, beneath and around the moody grandeur of Table Mountain, is without doubt one of the loveliest in the southern hemisphere. Cape Town's port is quieter than it was in the heyday of the passenger steamer. And other harbours, much closer to the northern industrial markets, have poached much of its freight traffic. Marine and mercantile enterprises still contribute substantially to the local economy, though. Its wider base includes light engineering and manufacturing, the service industries and tourism – the beaches, the attractive wineland-and-mountain hinterland, the history in the stones of the buildings, the calendar of arts, the eating and drinking places, and the undemanding, unhurried lifestyle are powerful attractions. A great many people retire to or near the city. The Peninsula is 1 463 kilometres from Johannesburg, 1 716 kilometres from Durban, and its residents sometimes tend to feel left out of things.

■ It is difficult to say with certainty whether *Port Elizabeth* or Durban is South Africa's second-oldest city. Probably Port Elizabeth, which is where the 1820 Settlers set their optimistic feet ashore. It is now a great port, but it took decades to grow into anything resembling such. But the place did eventually develop (it formally became a city in 1913) into an impressive modern complex of dockyards, motor assembly plants, factories and commercial buildings sustaining, together with its satellites of Uitenhage and Kirkwood, some half-million economically active people. Port Elizabeth was especially hard hit by the recessions of the mid-1980s and early 1990s.

Not far away from Port Elizabeth is the historic city of Grahamstown, familiarly known as the 'city of saints' because of its many churches. Overlooked by the impressive 1820 British Settlers' Monument, home of Rhodes University and several famous schools, Grahamstown, keeper of English South Africa's soul, is among the most attractive of the country's smaller centres.

■ *Durban*, on the Natal coast and third-largest of the cities is aptly known as 'South Africa's playground', though it is more reminiscent of Blackpool than of Cannes. Durban is not, however, the capital of Natal: that honour belongs to the pretty little city of Pietermaritzburg some 90 kilometres inland.

Durban's origins, and its history, are very English. It started life as the trading and white-hunter outpost of Port Natal when, in 1824, the enterprising Lieutenant Farewell of the good ship *Julia* (he had previously served on the *Beagle* of Darwinian fame) disembarked 40 white settlers, to whom the Zulu king Shaka, with surprising benevolence, granted 9 000 square kilometres of rich land around the bay. Progress was slow at first (in 1835 there were still only 30 or so residents), but with the launching of immigration schemes in the 1840s the town expanded rapidly. Today, more than a million and a half people inhabit the Durban-Pinetown complex; its 1 668-hectare bay area has 15 195 metres of quayside that handles bulk cargoes of, among other commodities, grain, coal, manganese, and sugar from the plantations. The local industrial and commercial base is broad; food-processing and, predictably, marine-orientated businesses such as warehousing and oil storage being prominent.

■ *Durban-Pinetown* is said to be the world's fastest-growing conurbation, its population expanding faster than those of Calcutta and Mexico City – but expanding for much the same reasons. The armies of the poor have been leaving a countryside that can no longer meet their minimum needs, and are congregating in their thousands around Ntujuma, Umlazi, Embumbula and other ramshackle settlements on the western city fringes. Their integration into the urban mainstream, the provision of jobs, houses, schools, clinics – these are the Durban's real priorities, and the contrast between the reality and the image the city projects – that of a playground for the privileged – is marked indeed. But then, it is only by exploiting its considerable natural assets to the full, by offering the ultimate in frivolous pleasure, that Durban can remain prosperous enough to cope with the future.

Greater Durban is also home to large numbers of Indian people, many of them direct descendants of the indentured labourers brought in during the 1860s to work the great sugar plantations of the region (see page 12).

■ *Bloemfontein*, capital of the Orange Free State and judicial capital of the Republic of South Africa, sprawls over 16 900 hectares of dry, treeless central plateau countryside.

It is largely an administrative city (though it has 350 or so light industries, and the largest railway workshops in the country) – around 40 per cent of its economically active citizens are employed in social, community or government services. The town has some fine buildings, notably the 19th-century republican Raadsaal, or parliament – a dignified mix of Renaissance form and Classical-revival detail – and the splendid new Opera House that was completed in 1985.

■ *Pretoria*, State administrative capital and a place of some one million souls, is known as the 'jacaranda city' because of the 70 000 or so lovely lilac-blossomed trees that grace the gardens, parks and about 650 kilometres of well-laid-out streets. The city has a magnificent setting, overlooked by hills on which the renowned architect Herbert Baker placed his Union Buildings, model for the grander but no more pleasing seat of the Raj government in New Delhi. There are other impressive structures, especially the turn-of-the-century Palace of Justice, described as 'one of the finest classical public spaces in South Africa'. Church Square has always been Pretoria's hub, but nowadays is not a very attractive one. At the time of Union it could have become one of the architectural glories of the subcontinent, embellished with fountains and flowers and Continental-style paving (this was the citizenry's preference). Instead, the civic authorities chose to redesign it as a tramway terminus. Says author Vivien Allen: 'Pretoria exchanged its heart for a public transport system.'

■ Sixty kilometres south of Pretoria is the financial and industrial epicentre of South Africa: the *Witwatersrand*, with the high-rise density of Johannesburg at its centre.

The Witwatersrand has an inner and an outer ring of towns. The former, around metropolitan Johannesburg, comprises the largely dormitory municipalities of Sandton (rich, chic, and pretentious), Randburg, Roodepoort, Edenvale, Germiston, Alberton (the last two somewhat downmarket), Bedfordview and Soweto, the largest black urban complex in the country. The outer zone includes the substantial centres of Krugersdorp (Dr Jameson's Waterloo – see page 27), Randfontein, Westonaria, Kempton Park (which has a fine racetrack), Benoni, Springs and Boksburg.

These towns are built on gold, discovered just a hundred years ago (see page 27), which still sustains them but not by any means exclusively – about 50 per cent of the entire country's gross product is generated by the huge number of mining, manufacturing, commercial and financial enterprises in the area.

Nobody can pretend Johannesburg is a beautiful city. It is notably lacking in open spaces; the mine-dumps are an eyesore (though most of them now have thin coats of greenery; an improvement on the dust-blown past). But there is a vibrancy, a bustling, honestly materialistic vitality about the place that does have its appeal. And it has a marvellous climate: it is situated high on the central plateau where the air is rare and heady, the winters clear and not too cold, the summer heat (in good years) relieved by late-afternoon rainstorms that are often cloudbursts of Lear-like proportions. On average Johannesburg gets more rain in four summer months than England's notoriously soggy Manchester does in a full year.

DE BEERS MINE, 1872.

BOER AGAINST BRITON. The discovery of diamonds in the northern Cape in the late 1860s and of massive deposits of gold on the Witwatersrand in 1886 fuelled the engine of Imperial expansionism and threatened the independence of the two northern Boer republics. The result: two major wars, the second and more devastating triggered by, among other events, Dr Jameson's provocative raid into the Transvaal on New Year's Day, 1897.

This period also saw the last and greatest of the black backlashes against nineteenth-century colonial conquest.

The Battle of Isandlwana in 1879 (1) where the large British force was virtually annihilated by Cetshwayo's Zulu army. Household Cavalry showing the flag (2) after the annexation of the Transvaal, an event which led directly to the Transvaal War of 1880-81 and another humiliating British defeat, this one on the bloody slopes of Majuba Hill (7).

The diamond-rich Big Hole at Kimberley, 1872 (3). Paul Kruger (4), patriarchal President of the South African Republic (the Transvaal), and (5) his arch-enemy in the corridors of southern African power, the ruthless visionary Cecil Rhodes. Hordes of prospectors – *uitlanders,* or foreigners – descended on the northern territories in the 1870s and 1880s (6).

The gulf between Briton and Boer became an unbridgeable chasm after the Jameson Raid, and the Anglo-Boer War erupted three years later. The relief of Boer-besieged Ladysmith, February 1900 (8). Boer hit-and-run tactics (9) succeeded in protracting hostilities for a further 18 exhausting months. Christiaan de Wet (11) was one of the most gifted of the guerrilla leaders. British commander-in-chief Kitchener replied with scorched earth, barbed wire, blockhouse and concentration camp. Pictured are displaced Boer women *en route* to internment (10). Peace at last: Generals Louis Botha and Kitchener after the Treaty of Vereeniging (12).

THE PAST

Often in the telling, perhaps too often, South Africa's story begins with a tiny band of hardy seventeenth-century Dutchmen making their landfall beneath the grandeur of Table Mountain, on the southern tip of the subcontinent, to create the first permanent white settlement of Francis Drake's 'fairest cape'.

That was of course the first really significant landmark in the annals of the modern, structured state, but for millennia before southern Africa had been home to darker-skinned people. Archaeological finds indicate that the ancestors of the San, or Bushmen, populated the northern part of the subcontinent as long as 30 000 years ago. They were small bands of nomadic hunter-gatherers who roamed the great sunlit spaces in search of sustenance and solitude, a unique culture that once flourished but has now all but disappeared. For a protracted time, throughout the Later Stone Age, they were the dominant people in the vast area that stretched from today's Namibia eastwards to KwaZulu-Natal and from the Limpopo to Agulhas on the stormy southern Cape coast.

Not that the word 'dominant', and all that it suggests, is appropriate in the context of San society. Entirely without hostility, these gentle, extraordinary people had – still have – a profound belief in sharing: in co-operation with the family, between clan and clan, between man and his environment. Custom and conviction excluded personal antagonism; nature, both animate and inanimate, was sanctified, hallowed in the mystic rituals of the hunt and the trance-like dance, and in the lively cave-paintings and engravings that grace some 2 000 recorded sites throughout southern Africa.

Later on came other peoples, succeeding migratory waves that washed southwards to mingle with, sometimes to fight against and eventually displace, the San.

One of the first of these groups were the Khoikhoi (Hottentots) or 'men of men' as they called themselves – who, although related to the small-statured hunters of the plains, were pastoralists, herders of cattle living in fairly well-organized tribal groupings and conscious of territorial rights. These were the people with whom the explorers and circumnavigators of Portugal and England, France and Holland first came into contact on the shores of the Cape, a meeting that usually resulted in mutually profitable barter but occasionally in deadly combat.

The Bantu-speaking people were comparative late-comers. They are believed to have originated in West Africa, and began to filter across the Limpopo River in about 200 AD, settling in parts of what is now the Northern Transvaal. A second group, with a more advanced Later Iron Age culture, began to arrive in the subcontinent some time after the year 1200. By the time the first Cape Europeans started putting down their roots the Bantu-speakers were well established in many parts of the subcontinent.

Much of the story of black migration is shrouded in mystery, and theories are numerous and complex. It is generally agreed, though, that four main groups were involved: the Sotho, the Nguni, the Tsonga and the Venda. By the late seventeenth century their spearhead, the Xhosa (of the southern Nguni group), were well established in the eastern Cape, on a direct collision course with the expanding white farming communities. Inevitably, competition for living space would lead to bitter conflict. Inevitably, too, the Bushman population would be depleted almost to the point of extinction through the encroachment of better organized, more numerous, more warlike people – black tribes with refined military systems and, because they kept livestock and tilled the soil, an appetite for land.

Some Bushman groups were simply wiped out, the men killed and, often, the women taken captive, so introducing their genes into a substantial part of the subcontinent's ethnic composition (and into its culture; the 'click' in some of the languages and many of the animistic beliefs of traditional black societies are of Bushman origin). Others took a coastal lifestyle, forsaking the fruits of the hunt for those of the sea. Yet others, were left alone to pursue their ancient ways because they had made their homes in the immensity of the northern wastelands, the Kalahari regions, in which only they, with their simple needs and special skills, could survive.

The other branch of the family, the Khoikhoi, virtually ceased to exist as a coherent society after white settlement. Many, probably most, succumbed to savage outbreaks of smallpox and other alien epidemics of the eighteenth century. Some of the survivors moved inland to become the half-breed Korana, Griqua, and Oorlam groups. Others remained as 'Colonial Hottentots' and, after the abolition of slavery in the 1830s, mixed with the new freemen, adding their progeny to what eventually became known as the Cape coloured community. Today only a few groups, notably the Nama people of the south-western region of the country and in Namibia, retain an identity clearly traceable to their Khoikhoi origins.

THE COMING OF THE WHITE MAN

In August 1487 two 100-ton caravels and a small store-ship, under the command of Bartholomeu Dias, hoisted full sail in the mouth of the Tagus River and set a south-westerly course into the Atlantic. Sixteen months later Dias was back in Portugal, without any great treasures but with the certain and profoundly valuable knowledge that his ships had rounded the southern tip of Africa. The sea-route to India and the spice-rich Molucca Islands was, at last, open to Portugal's royal fleets.

The curious probability is, though, that his epic voyage was not the first to have taken European explorers around the Cape. Some two thousand years earlier a flotilla of sturdy Phoenician biremes – double-banked galleys – almost certainly accomplished this feat. Their captains had been charged by Pharaoh Necho to sail down the east coast – that is to say, through the Red Sea and past Zanzibar – and to 'come back through the Pillars of Hercules to the Northern Sea and so to Egypt'.

This they duly did and reported, according to the Greek historian Herodotus, 'a thing which I cannot believe, but another man may, namely, in sailing round Libya [the ancient name for Africa], they had the sun on their right hand'. In other words they had coasted westwards past Cape Point.

However that may be, it was the Portuguese of the fifteenth and sixteenth centuries who, 'in the service of God our Lord and to our own advantage', pioneered the modern trade routes. Armed with the most rudimentary of navigational aids – a mariner's compass, instruments to gauge wind direction and an astrolabe to determine latitude – their talented admirals set out to find and chart the sea lane to the treasure-troves of the east. Diego Cão negotiated the arid Namib coast, reaching a point just to the north of present-day Swakopmund in 1486. Two years later Dias ran into the notorious Cape south-easter, allowed his ships to be driven a thousand miles and more into the Atlantic Ocean; then set course first southwards and finally north-east to make his landfall at Mossel Bay – a prodigious exercise in navigational acrobatics that had taken him past the Cape of Storms.

The way was now open, though Dias would enjoy little of the glory; at Algoa Bay, site of modern Port Elizabeth, the votes of his less intrepid travelling companions went against him and he was forced to turn back. It was left to the strong-willed, supremely confident Vasco da Gama, nine years later, to chart a course up the east coast to the busy Islamic outposts of Mozambique, where his 'ships of Franks' caused some consternation, and thence across the Indian Ocean to Malabar and beyond.

Thereafter, for over a century, the Iberian commercial empire (Portugal and Spain were unified by dynastic marriage in 1580) flourished, providing both a magnet for and a challenge to other, increasingly enterprising, maritime powers. Of these, certainly insofar as the Cape sea lanes to India were concerned, the Dutch were to emerge as the leaders.

For much of the sixteenth century the hard-headed merchants of the Netherlands acted as middlemen in the lucrative spice trade, distributing the precious merchandise throughout a Europe enjoying renascent prosperity, legitimate contributors to business life, welcomed by both supplier and customer.

Less legitimate were the freebooters, who scoured the seas in their swift, well-armed ships in search of the easy pickings provided by galleons heavily laden with wealth of the Indies and the Americas. But, generally speaking, relations between Antwerp and Lisbon remained amicable enough, until the last decade of the century. Then, for a number of reasons related to the unification of Portugal and Spain, the Dutch decided to go it alone, and to deal directly with the Spice Islands.

Successful reconnaissance expeditions were mounted in the 1590s by the brothers De Houtman and by Jan van Linschoten, whose five-year odyssey produced a rich volume of hitherto secret information on the Portuguese trade and trading regions, all of which he consolidated into his *Itinerario*, published in 1595 and soon to become a kind of mercantile and navigational bible for Holland's seafaring fraternity. Between 1595 and 1602 rival Dutch companies, now competing in earnest for the Moluccan connection, sent a series of fleets to the East Indies, their voyages involving a longer haul across the Indian Ocean than the traditional Portuguese route from Mozambique to Malabar on the Indian subcontinent. The Cape and its watering places therefore became increasingly significant in the calculations of the Dutch navigators.

Both Mossel Bay, which Da Gama had named *Angra de São Bras*, and Table Bay, known then as Saldanha Bay (the name now belongs to a rocky embayment some 100 kilometres to the north), had been used by Portuguese and other admirals for the previous hundred years as incidental ports of call, natural harbours where there was shelter from storms and where emergency repairs could be effected, fresh water taken from the perennial springs and provisions bought by barter.

Indeed, as early as 1501 one devout commander, João da Nova, had erected a small stone church at São Bras, the first European building to be constructed on what is now South African soil. It was to be half a century, though, before any Dutchman thought of establishing a permanent presence on the southern shore. In due course the competing interests within Holland's mercantile world sank their differences and united under the federal umbrella of the Dutch East India Company, formally incorporated, and granted its charter by the States General of the Netherlands in 1602. During the decades that followed, the Company, which had a directorate grandly known as 'The Lords Seventeen', created a maritime empire that elevated tiny Holland to the highest ranks of Europe's nation states. It established a sophisticated administration in the Malayan Archipelago and, after 1619, a permanent far-eastern headquarters at Batavia (Java), the whole supported by a spreading network of garrisoned trading stations called comptoirs.

The Company's decision to create a comptoir at the Cape was more the result of accident than forethought. In 1647 the *Nieuw Haerlem* foundered on the shores of Table Bay and, although the captain and most of the crew were taken on to Holland aboard another vessel – part of a fleet whose passenger-list included Jan van Riebeeck – some 60 sailors, under command of junior merchant Leendert Janszen, remained behind at the Cape, sheltered from the elements by a crude fort built of wood salvaged from the wreck.

On his return a full year later Janszen submitted his *Remonstrantie*, a report strongly urging the Company to establish a victualling post at the Cape: a station that would trade peaceably with the local Khoikhoi (Hottentot) community, and supply fresh produce to the scurvy-ridden crews of ships bound to and from the East Indies.

On the strength of Janszen's submission, and a carefully argued second opinion by Jan van Riebeeck – the 32-year-old former Company employee who had walked the slopes of Table Mountain a year before and who was now anxious to re-enter Company service – the decision was taken. Scarcely a momentous one in the context of the Dutch East India Company's overall, immense operations – just another small fort manned by a hundred or so men, and this one at the southern end of an unknown land that, according to one jaundiced seafarer, 'yielded nothing to delight the heart of man'. Van Riebeeck was appointed commander, and his instructions drawn up. Modestly, and without fanfare, the expedition sailed out of Texel on 24 December 1651.

THE FIRST SETTLEMENT

In the practical, somewhat prosaic minds of the Lords Seventeen there was no thought of colonizing the Cape, let alone a vision of creating a European Christian state on the African continent. Their aims were commercial and limited. Nevertheless, a century and a half after the landing of Van Riebeeck, when the Dutch finally relinquished control, the makings of such a state did exist. The frontiers of white settlement had been pushed 500 kilometres to the east and 100 kilometres of prosperous farmland and vineyards lay to the north and north-east.

By the year 1806, when the British assumed control of the Cape for the second time, Cape Town was a busy seaport, host to ships of a score of nations and the seat of a sophisticated administration. South Africa was a reality – an uncomfortable one, even then, for the clash of cultures, a foretaste of future conflict, was already in evidence. There was antagonism between Boer and Briton, between black and white and, always, the competitive struggle for land. The process had been put in motion, and was irreversible.

Nor did Van Riebeeck, the first commander, have aspirations beyond his immediate, functional task. His instructions, which he carried out with solid Dutch thoroughness, were quite specific: he was to provide for passing ships of the Company 'the means of procuring herbs, flesh, water and other needful refreshments – and by this means restore the health of the sick'. He was also to build a fort 'in order to take possession at the Cape and so that you cannot be surprised by anyone'.

Van Riebeeck's three little vessels, *Drommedaris* (his flagship), the *Reijger* and the *Goede Hoop*, nosed their way into Table Bay on the blustery evening of 6 April 1652.

Three days later the Commander had personally marked out the fort's site, and by 21 April the first rough walls had been erected and supported five cannons. The project, however, was to be plagued by set-back after set-back – the eastern ramparts simply could not withstand the driving rainstorms.

While the fort was being built, the Garden was also taking shape. The Cape is not always at its best in April and May: the settlers had to dig and build in downpours of icy rain which ruined most of the crops. Caterpillars and blight put paid to the rest. And not only did plants succumb to disease: dysentery, together with a number of other ailments, attacked the small community. There were Khoikhoi raids. Life was precarious.

But the chain of catastrophes came to an end, and fortune at last began to smile on the exiles. Sheep and cattle began to breed. Lemon and apple trees, brought by the relieving fleet, were planted, and for those more interested in the elixir of the grape and hop, the Cape's first tavern – run by Annetje Boom, wife of the settlement's chief gardener – opened. It did not lack for customers.

Among Van Riebeeck's terms of reference was an instruction from the directors of the Dutch East India Company to cultivate the friendship and co-operation of the local inhabitants, and to his credit he did manage to create a mutually profitable and generally amiable relationship with them.

The Peninsula Khoikhoi were divided into three fairly distinct groupings. The first to come into daily contact with the white settlers were the *Strandlopers* (or 'Beachrangers'), more correctly termed the *Goringhaicona* (which means 'children of the Goringhaiqua'), who tended to subsist on roots, the fruits of the sea and the few sheep they kept. Led by Harry Autshumao and numbering just a few dozen, they were not a notably homogeneous people, being bound more by shared poverty than by bonds of kinship. Larger, more prosperous and generally more sophisticated were the Gorachouqua and the Goringhaiqua, semi-nomadic clans who kept livestock and lived, albeit in temporary fashion, in reed huts, and who manufactured metal jewellery and cultivated tobacco. It was with these wealthier groups that the colonists bartered copper, iron, brass, alcohol, beads, knives and salt for fresh meat. Farther inland, to the north and west of the Peninsula, were the powerful Cochoqua people. The Khoikhoi proved hospitable enough, gregarious, eager for trade and quick to adopt the white man's ways. As early as 1656 the Commander could record that 'they are learning to speak Dutch fairly well...' Inevitably, territorial encroachment – by free-burgher and later by trekboer – did lead to sporadic friction: there were raids and two minor 'wars' (in 1659 and between 1673 and 1677). Nevertheless, by the end of the century the two races had reached some sort of *modus vivendi*, and many Khoikhoi, dispossessed of their traditional grazing lands, were in employment on farms and in town.

Jan van Riebeeck left the Cape for Batavia in 1662 and was succeeded by Commander Zacharias Wagenaar. Four years later, the building of Cape Town's sturdy Castle began. It was to be a full decade before the stronghold was complete, even though, in the early stages, pretty well everyone helped in the work, including the Commander himself, his wife and small son, who carried baskets of earth to the ramparts. At the end of the first day's work a feast was given during which one of the settlers read a poem to the effect that neither Augustus nor Julius Caesar had laid, as they had done that day, 'a cornerstone at the far end of the earth'.

PUTTING DOWN ROOTS

Among the Company's many injunctions to Van Riebeeck, one proved especially difficult to accommodate in the first years of the settlement – that it should be self-supporting. As the workload increased, so more officials arrived, putting such severe pressure on the community's modest larder that within two years ships anchored in Table Bay were off-loading more supplies than they were taking on.

Van Riebeeck's solution represented a radical change in policy: he turned to private enterprise, releasing a number of men from their Company contracts to set themselves up as independent farmers and tradesmen. Other 'free-burgher' families arrived from Holland. The results were immediate and gratifying. In its very first, experimental, year – 1656 – the block of land set aside at Rondebosch produced a bumper crop of wheat, enough for local needs with some to spare. A small beginning, perhaps, but a significant one – the Cape was now no longer a commercial garrison with strictly limited objectives but a permanent colony capable of growth. The move marked the start of the settlement proper.

Over the years the free-burghers grew in number, steadily pushing out the frontiers – to the Hottentots Holland region in the 1670s and to Stellenbosch nine years later. This charming little centre was named after Simon van der Stel, the outstandingly innovative Governor of the Cape from 1679 to the century's end. He had earmarked the district as an ideal wheat-producing area, and the farms which were established there paid such handsome dividends that within a short while there was an over-supply of corn and the emphasis was shifted to the growing of grapes and the making of wine.

Not that this was a new idea: Jan van Riebeeck himself took a deep interest in viticulture and, a mere month after setting foot ashore in 1652, had placed an order with Amsterdam for seeds and plants 'and also vines which ought to thrive as well on local hill slopes as they do in Spain and France'. He received his stock and by 2 February 1659 was able to confide to his journal that 'Today, praise be to God, wine can be made for the first time from Cape Grapes, namely from the new must fresh from the vat'. The first vineyard, on his private farm Boschheuvel (now Bishopscourt), contained just 12 000 vines; 30 years later the grape harvests had spread their gracious mantle over much of the hinterland. By 1750 there were four million vines growing around the pretty towns of Stellenbosch, Paarl and Franschhoek, yielding an annual flow of 12 000 hectolitres of wine.

People came to make their home in the new land. Most of them were Dutch, though there was a sprinkling of Belgians, Scandanavians and, especially, Germans. By the time the whites of the Cape numbered around a thousand, in 1688, they were joined by a group of most welcome immigrants – the sober and industrious Huguenots. These were French Protestants who, after the Edict of Nantes was revoked and they were threatened with religious persecution, fled to pastures new and far. There were 164 of them; a fine shot-in-the-arm for the small community.

The first Cape homes were modest, single-storeyed, flat-roofed affairs of sun-dried brick, the white-washed walls and green-painted woodwork lending a certain charm to the town. In the country areas the settlers built more substantial homes, often of stone, reed-thatched, thick-walled and functional. With prosperity, though, a distinctive style began to evolve during the latter part of the century: gabled, half-shuttered houses, the entrance-way an impressive focal point through which one walked into a spacious *voorhuis*. These farmsteads were built symmetrically, even severely, to 'T', 'H' and 'U' patterns. As the decades passed, the cold lines of the grander ones were softened with the addition of wings, and courtyards were encircled by outbuildings. Thus emerged the renowned Cape Dutch architectural idiom, some lovely examples of which still grace the Peninsula and particularly its northern and eastern hinterland.

With time, too, the gable changed, taking on a bewildering variety of shapes, plain and rounded giving way to convoluted convex-concave; to classical; and to the elaborately ornate, thick edge-mouldings sweeping across in swirls and scrolls and curlicues. Eventually, and unhappily, this most distinctive of architectural features became little more than an ugly and irrelevant appendage to the worst kind of run-of-the-mill South African suburban home.

Curiously enough, many of the early architectural elements, including the gable, derived not from Holland but from the East and were introduced by Malay slaves skilled in building crafts. Slavery, indeed, was a prominent aspect of Cape community life for almost 200 years. The early settlers were inhibitively short of labour, both skilled and unskilled: Van Riebeeck, as we've seen, was unable to conscript the local Khoikhoi, and a formal decision to import slaves was taken in the 1660s.

The system was an iniquitous one in retrospect, but not exclusive to the Cape: slave-trading and owning was common practice in much of the world until the 1830s and later; across the Atlantic a civil war was fought over the issue in the 1860s. The first slave to appear was a stowaway from Batavia who arrived at the Cape in March 1653, but slavery really began five years later when, in 1658, the *Amersfoort* acquired 170 slaves from a Portuguese ship and off-loaded them at Table Bay.

Thereafter, demand from wheat- and wine-farming free-burghers ensured a steady growth in numbers, despite the cost (up to 100 *gulden* per slave) and the high incidence of runaways. By 1710 there were about 1 200 adult slaves at the Cape; in 1795, when the British took over, the figure had risen to 17 000 – a number somewhat in excess of the white population. They were brought, originally, from places as far afield as Guinea and Angola on Africa's west coast, Delagoa Bay on the east, as well as from Madagascar, Java and, especially, Malaya.

After the initial influx, importation dwindled to a trickle: children born to slave parents accounted for the steady growth rate.

THE ROAD TO THE EAST

Like any frontier community, the early Cape Settlers had their share of enterprising explorers. Forays into the northern interior were launched by Wintervogel (who reached present-day Malmesbury); Gabbema (the Berg River Valley and Paarl, which he named after the giant granite boulders that dominate the area – depending on the light they often gleam like pearls); Danckaert (the Cederberg and Olifants River – named for a herd of 300 elephant he saw); Van Meerhoff (Namaqualand). Van der Stel himself led an expedition to the copper mountains of Namaqualand in 1685. A hundred years after Van Riebeeck's landing Jacobus Coetsee, a captain of the burgher dragoons, crossed the Orange River and wandered over the high plateau for some months. The eastern horizons were broadened by, among others, Hieronimus Cruse in the late 1660s: he trekked overland to Mossel Bay and heard tell of 'darker-skinned men' – that is to say, the Xhosa, who were by then long settled along the east coast and were advancing southwards. Shortly afterwards the settlers got to know more about these mysterious black people with the stranding, in 1686, of the Dutch ship *Stavenisse* south of the future Port Natal on the east coast: the rescue parties produced eyewitness accounts of the Xhosa around the Kei River.

Settlement of the eastern districts received its first major impetus when, in 1699, Governor Willem Adriaan van der Stel (Simon's second son) reversed Company policy, which had hitherto discouraged stock-farmers from trekking. Throughout the eighteenth century the frontiers were pushed steadily outwards to the north

and east by the relentless advance of trekboers – nomadic farmers moving farther away from the restrictions of government. New magisterial districts, each controlled by an official known as a *landdrost*, were established as the virgin land was tamed and homesteads were built.

In 1745 a new *drostdy* – as the regional headquarters of the *landdrost* were called – was established in the attractive little village which, two years later, was to be named Swellendam. By midcentury the boundary of the Cape of Good Hope had reached the Great Brak River near Mossel Bay and farms were appearing as far away as the west bank of the Gamtoos. By the 1780s settlers had moved farther eastwards and were putting down their roots along the Great Fish River; before the decade was out the town and district of Graaff-Reinet had been formally proclaimed. By this time the central administration in Cape Town was at acrimonious odds with the farther reaches of its eastern domains. Ruggedly individualistic frontiersmen, resenting distant and what they regarded as misguided control over their economic life, and the Company's handling of the Xhosa problem, declared (briefly) their own independent republics; Graaff-Reinet in February 1795 and Swellendam four months later.

In fact the physical power of the Dutch East India Company, and therefore the strength of its administrative muscle in the regions, had been declining since the early 1700s. Towards the end of the century, after four debilitating Anglo-Dutch wars, France and England had emerged as the leading European protagonists, rivals in the quest for, among other things, control of the oceans. The Cape, weakly garrisoned and strategically positioned on the sea-routes, was a tempting prize. British troops landed at Muizenberg in July 1795, but six weeks were to pass before the local militia could be defeated at Wynberg Hill. The capitulation, signed at Rondebosch on 16 September, inaugurated a period of direct rule from Whitehall that, with one brief break, was to underpin events on the subcontinent for the next hundred years and more – until the Act of Union of 1910 created the all-but-sovereign state of South Africa.

THE BRITISH PRESENCE

The country that the English soldiers took over was still very much a backwater in the flow of international affairs. True, Cape Town had grown, but at the end of the eighteenth century it still comprised little more than a cluster of 2 000 or so houses that sprawled from the jettied dockside up and around the lower slopes of Table Mountain. Along the Liesbeeck River there were a few still-rural villages that were later to become the swathe of suburbia stretching from Woodstock to Wynberg; farther afield lay a hinterland of prosperous wheat and wine farms, and the remote and troubled eastern border area.

The town itself was attractive enough, its pride the Gardens, started by Van Riebeeck as a prosaic vegetable patch but now assuming a more decorative rôle. Indeed as early as 1685 the visiting scholar Abbé de Choisy could observe that he 'would have liked to see it in a corner of Versailles'. Oaks and ashes shaded its more mundane plants; a pleasure lodge had been added in 1700 (later, some think, rebuilt to become Government House, now known as the Tuynhuis). There was a menagerie at the mountain end; fine buildings, including the Old Supreme Court, which had started life as the Slave Lodge, had made their appearance.

Leading from harbour to garden was the elegant, stone-paved, oaklined Heerengracht – present-day Adderley Street. The land beyond the quaint old harbour area was much later to be reclaimed from the sea and now supports many of Cape Town's modern city blocks and dockland.

Other features contributed substance and, if not sophistication, certainly charm to the place: the leisurely spaciousness of the

THE AGE OF THE GENERALS. In 1910 the two former republics of the Transvaal and the Orange Free State came together with the British colonies of the Cape and Natal to form the Union of South Africa, and for the next four decades – years of war abroad and sporadic rebellion at home, of both economic depression and industrial progress – the political arena was dominated by three Afrikaners, all of whom had fought with distinction against the British during the Anglo-Boer War. Louis Botha and Jan Smuts were statesmen, 'Empire men' who practised the politics of reconciliation; Barry Hertzog a dedicated nationalist whose ideological heirs would eventually, in 1948, grasp and hold the reins of power on behalf of Afrikanerdom.

Members of the National Convention (1) which created the Union constitution. Union celebrations in Cape Town, 1910 (2). Mohandas Gandhi (3 *left*) laboured long, hard and with only partial success for Indian rights in South Africa. Alfred Lord Milner (4), architect of the Anglo-Boer War and chief engineer of a post-war reconstruction programme that paved the way for a united South Africa. Black land rights and taxation were the elements that triggered the Bambata Rebellion – an uprising of some 6 000 Zulu people – in 1906. Colonial troops are pictured (5) executing rebels. General Louis Botha (6), the Union's first premier and commander-in-chief of its forces, with his staff during the First World War. Botha had first to quell an anti-British white rebellion at home before leading his army in the conquest of German South West Africa: picture (8) shows the raising of the Union Jack over the Rathaus at Windhoek. Mounted police clear Rissik Street, Johannesbrug (9) during the 1922 'Red Revolt', a violent reaction by white miners to the threat posed by cheap black labour on the Witwatersrand. Barry Hertzog (7). In 1939 South Africa again joined the Allied cause against Germany, her troops – all volunteers – campaigning successfully in East Africa, the Western Desert and Italy. Shown here is a recruiting station in Adderley Street, Cape Town (10). Field Marshal Smuts at No. 10 Downing Street (11) with Winston Churchill shortly after the German surrender on 8 May 1945.

Grand Parade; some beautiful private residences, the Cape style perhaps best exemplified by the pleasantly solid Koopmans de Wet House on Strand Street; the massive Castle on what was then the waterfront, and of course the town's busy, warren-like dockland. Cape Town had become one of the foremost ports of the southern hemisphere, host to ships and sailors of a dozen nations and already famed as the 'tavern of the seas', its clubs and pubs proliferating, its streets alive with horse-drawn traffic and the press of polyglot humanity.

Indeed, as colonial headquarters went, the new British administrators could have been a great deal worse off. They settled themselves in comfortably after the second occupation, in 1806, and addressed the issues of government: slavery; the growing spirit of independence among the Boers of the outlying regions; the agitated Xhosa presence on the eastern border; the need to economize (Britain had incurred a huge war debt during the Napoleonic struggles), and sparseness of the frontier settler community.

In 1806 the colony's population comprised 26 000 whites, some 30 000 slaves, 20 000 Khoikhoi and uncountable numbers of Bushmen and Bantu-speaking people beyond the Great Fish River, posing a constant threat to the tiny border farming settlements.

The first full-scale Frontier War had erupted in 1779; altogether, there would be eight more over the next hundred years and during this time the border was moved progressively eastwards to the Kei River. Of these series of frontier skirmishes, probably the most significant was the fifth, in 1819, when the Xhosa army mounted a direct attack on Grahamstown. This was repulsed by the garrison but the event convinced Governor Lord Charles Somerset that only massive immigration could bring any semblance of stability to the troubled border areas.

Conviction was translated into action with the landing in Algoa Bay, in 1820, of 60 parties of English, Scots and Irish families numbering some 4 000 men, women and children – a small fraction of the 90 000 who had applied to emigrate but enough, the authorities decided, to populate and pacify the recently proclaimed Albany district of the eastern Cape – the vast area covering most of the disputed territory between the Bushmans and Great Fish Rivers and from Grahamstown to the coast.

From Algoa Bay the newcomers were moved inland by ox-wagon (at their own expense) in blissful ignorance of the almost impossible conditions that awaited them. Warning bells sounded clear, however, when they took leave of Colonel Cuyler, *landdrost* (magistrate) of Uitenhage, who had accompanied them part of the way. 'Gentlemen', he said, 'when you go out to plough, never leave your guns at home.' It dawned on them that they were to serve not only as pioneers but also as a kind of plain-clothes militia, and in a short while they would also discover that battle with the desolate land would test their courage and endurance even more than that against the Xhosa.

Their troubles were complex and legion, perhaps most poignantly summed up in a letter from one Captain Buller, written during the first season. He said: 'My wheat, two months ago the most promising I ever saw in any country, is now cut down and in heaps for burning ... The rust has utterly destroyed it; not a grain have we saved. My barley, from the drought, and a grub which attacks the blade, produced little more than I sowed. My Indian corn, very much injured by the caterpillar; cabbages destroyed by the lice; the beans all scorched by the hot wind ... Our cows are all dry from want of grass; not the least appearance of verdure as far as the eye can reach. Nothing but one great wilderness of faded grass. On Saturday whilst watching by the sick bed of my dear little girl (she had been bitten by a snake while running over the veld without shoes and stockings, and died), I was startled by the cry of wild dogs. I ran to the window and saw about thirty of these ferocious

animals; before I could drive them off, they had killed twenty of my flock, which consisted of twenty-seven in all. I stood for a moment thinking of my misery, my dying child, my blasted crops, my scattered and ruined flock. God's will be done. I have need of fortitude to bear up against such accumulation of misery. Farewell ...'

The settlers suffered five years of bitter hardship and disappointment on the unforgiving land: conditions were primitive; equipment rudimentary; the allotments too small; the ban on recruiting labour from among the Xhosa clans a prohibitive restriction; the depredations of drought, locust and tribesman an unrelenting menace. Few survived as farmers, most of them drifting into the villages and small towns, originally military garrisons, that now studded the eastern Cape countryside.

Nevertheless, the pioneer scheme was not a total failure in the context of the British colonial administration's priorities, high among which was the creation of a white-inhabited 'buffer' region in the east. Four thousand new settlers might not seem a very substantial number by modern standards, but it increased the area's population by a full ten per cent. Moreover, things improved dramatically in the decade after 1825. It saw more freedom of movement, bigger farms and a general relaxation of bureaucratic restriction and the introduction, by the settlers, of a sheep-farming industry that was to become the country's principal agricultural activity and the mainstay of the eastern Cape economy, ushered in a welcome era of prosperity and growth.

Towards the end of the 1830s, too, an organized community of Britons put its first, tentative roots down on the far eastern coast.

Since 1834 there had been a small trading post at Port Natal – founded by the enterprising Lieutenant Francis Farewell – and white hunters stalked the thickly wooded hinterland in search of elephant and ivory. They were tolerated, even welcomed, by the powerful Zulu king Shaka. They were transients rather than colonists, even if they did hold land – 9 000 square kilometres around the bay – under a royal, though vague, grant. The status of the settlement changed with the arrival of the missionary and magistrate Allen Gardiner, who called a meeting on 23 June 1835 to proclaim a township. At the inaugural get-together, Gardiner remembered, 'almost total silence was observed ... At length a voice cried out: "Now let's go and settle the bounds" ... Being the winter season, it was a sort of union of hunters, who, tired of chasing sea-cows and buffalo, were now sighing for town houses and domestic cheer ...'

It was in this casual, impromptu fashion that Durban, later to become South Africa's premier port and third city, was founded. During the course of the nineteenth century, large-scale immigration schemes ensured both its growth and Natal's quintessentially English character, but for the first decade or so the settlement remained small and vulnerable, its affairs intimately bound up with the eastern prong of the Great Trek.

THE OUTWARD URGE

In the mid-1830s there began an exodus of Boers from the volatile eastern Cape. Families gathered in parties, inspanned their oxen and headed into the immense and little-known northern and northeastern interior armed with scarcely more than musket, Bible and faith in their destiny.

The migration, apparently spontaneous in its initial thrust but in fact well organized, started in a modest way, gathered momentum over the next few turbulent years and eventually, when the sound of battle had died away and the wanderers became farmers again, succeeded in doubling the area of white settlement in Africa.

Arguments about the nature of the Great Trek are numerous and conflicting. To the dispassionate historian it was just one more movement of peoples in search of *lebensraum* in a century characterized by mass-migrations, comparable perhaps to the westward advance of the American pioneers. To the Afrikaners it remains a heroic saga, fount of their republican traditions and of their national identity. To British officialdom of the time and later it was a catastrophe, the origin of a divided country: the trigger for deep and lasting dissension between Boer, Briton and black people. To blacks the Trek must have appeared simply as a blatant exercise in physical conquest. What is not in dispute is that, in the end, the Afrikaner nation did manage to occupy huge territories between the Orange and the Limpopo, to establish independent republics and, ultimately, to wage a long and bitter war against the British Empire. It was, without doubt, the most crucial event in the story of modern South Africa.

Much has been said of the Trek's causes: of the ruinous losses suffered by Boer homesteaders in the exposed eastern frontier region during their never-ending struggle for land against the Xhosa; of lack of military support from the British authorities in Cape Town; of the colonial government's 'over-reactive' respect for the status and rights of black people, inspired by philanthropists in London and Scottish missionaries in Africa; of the abolition of slavery; and above all of British meddling in and control over the affairs of independent-minded frontiersmen. The essence of the whole matter was more simply, if rather ruggedly, explained to an English resident of Bathurst in the 1830s. The Boer said that 'in his father's lifetime and his own they had been five times clean swept out by [Xhosa raiders] ... but in those old times when they were robbed they redressed the matter themselves, but now their hands were tied while [the Xhosa's] were loose'.

There was, though, a more positive side: the Boer people were not simply running away from an intolerable situation, they were moving towards what they perceived as their Promised Land. They knew a little of what lay in the vast interior; earlier migrants had preceded them, individual *trekboers* who had wandered the northern veld for generations in search of better grazing and hunting-grounds. From the information that filtered back the prospects of finding peace and solitude appeared bright enough to merit exploration, if for no other reason than that many of the eastern and northern regions had been subjected to the brutal ravages of what is known as the *Difaqane*, a cataclysm that had drastically reduced the size of many of the indegenous populations and had distorted and weakened traditional inter-tribal affiliations, both of which factors, for different reasons, tended to encourage intrusive settlement.

To digress a little from the Great Trek (though the two events were closely interactive), the *Difaqane*, in its simplest definition, was the forced migration of millions of black tribesmen, initially to the west and north of Zululand and eventually over most of the northern subcontinent. It began when Shaka, leader of the Zulus and warrior supreme, cleared his immediate neighbourhood of all opposition and set out on the bloody road of conquest, helping to ignite a massive chain reaction of violence and counter-violence. Other disruptive forces were also at work, notably the slave raiders of the Mozambique seaboard and the colonial British of the eastern Cape, whose advance into Xhosa country led to dispossession, and migration, on a significant scale. Defeated tribes would move on, displacing others, who in turn migrated to spread fire, sword and famine in farther reaches. It was the domino principle in classic and devastating action. To cite three examples:

■ Shaka launched his first attack on Matiwane's powerful Ngwane clan in the eastern foothills of the Drakensberg. Matiwane moved on southwards and westwards, to assault the southern Nguni and the Sotho of the uplands, who scattered to cause havoc elsewhere.
■ Mzilikazi, perhaps Shaka's most enterprising general, quarrelled with his king and fled north with an army that grew as he conquered and absorbed tribe after tribe. His cataclysmically destructive path led him to the Olifants River and then westwards into Sotho territory. Eventually he was defeated in the Transvaal by a mixed force of trekkers, Khoikhoi and Tswana, and moved on, across the Limpopo River, to establish the Matabele empire.

Two other groups were founded by disaffected Zulu commanders: Soshangane, who led his *impis* into Mozambique (the Sangaans); and Zwangendaba, who settled 2 000 kilometres to the north, around Lake Malawi (the Angoni).

Meanwhile, the Boers trekked, first in their hundreds and then in their thousands. The story is complex to the point where, certainly within the scope of this brief narrative, it defies meaningful synthesis. However, it can perhaps be divided into two broad segments:

First, a substantial element of the trekkers saw Natal as their ultimate haven. Groups of these crossed the Orange and, by the middle of 1837, had gathered at a place between Thaba Nchu and the Vet River from where an advance party, led by Piet Retief, set off eastwards towards Durban and beyond, into Zululand. Shaka's successor, Dingaan, received Retief with deceptive amiability and by December the main body of trekkers, encouraged by the promise of land south of the Tugela River, had hauled their wagons over the high Drakensberg, and were in Natal.

After concluding the formal treaty, however, Retief and his pathfinder party of 69 were murdered on the instructions of Dingaan, who went on to attack the trekkers in a series of fierce engagements at Bloukrans, Bushmans River and elsewhere.

The trekkers had suffered grievous casualties but by the end of 1838 they had managed to rally their forces. On 16 December, after a night spent in prayer and in the offering of the formal vow, or covenant, at a place now known as Blood River, their muskets and laagered discipline routed the Zulu army.

The Boer Republic of Natalia was destined to be short-lived. In May 1842 British troops occupying Durban were besieged by the Boers, but succeeded in summoning reinforcements (this was the occasion of Dick King's renowned 1 500-kilometre ride to enlist the help of the garrison of Grahamstown) and the four-year-old State disintegrated. Some of the Boers returned to the Cape; most rejoined the main body of northern Voortrekkers.

These had in the meantime been busy preparing the way for settlement of the land beyond the Orange River. During the next decade numerous small groups of hardy pioneers took their wagon-trains over enormous tracts of inhospitable country, suffering hardship, privation and, some of them, death along the way. Heat and drought, disease, the ravages of wild animals and confrontation with the black tribes, all took their toll. Andries Potgieter's party pushed the farthest north, crossing the Limpopo into present-day Zimbabwe as early as 1836. Van Rensburg's was annihilated in Mozambique. Louis Trichardt's odyssey took him first to the northern Transvaal's Soutpansberg and then south-east through fever-ridden Mozambique to Delagoa Bay (modern Maputo). Here both he and his wife died and the remnants of his decimated group took ship to Durban.

By the mid-1850s, however, the Boers had settled in sufficient numbers to warrant the establishment and formal recognition of two viable independent states, one between the Orange and the Vaal rivers, the other between the Vaal and the Limpopo.

TWO REPUBLICS, TWO COLONIES

From about the middle of the nineteenth century onwards southern Africa comprised four major and a number of less substantial political entities. They interacted, of course, but for the most part functioned separately, and continued to do so until Union in 1910. The web of events is intricate. In broad outline, however:

■ The country that was to become the Orange Free State – that is to say, the land between the Orange and the Vaal rivers – had been infiltrated by a few trekboers during the early pioneering years, but it was only with the northward advance of the Voortrekkers from 1835 that white-settlement began in earnest. The small township of Winburg (named in commemoration of the Boer victory over Mzilikazi's marauders at the Battle of Vegkop), was founded in 1837 as the 'capital' of the new territory. This decision turned out to be somewhat premature since the trekkers were still too divided to form a coherent state. Their lack of unity, and confusing element of black-white confrontation over land rights and frontiers, prompted the British to annex the area and to create the Orange River Sovereignty in 1848. Bloemfontein, then scarcely more than a schoolroom and a cluster of white-washed cottages, was declared the administrative centre and headquarters of the British Resident.

None of these events succeeded in bringing stability to the region (at one point the Boers rose in revolt, and were defeated by a force commanded by the Cape Governor, Sir Harry Smith). Finally, though, following the Bloemfontein Convention in 1854, Britain recognized the independence of the new Republic of the Orange Free State. Real progress was achieved under the steady guidance of Jan Brand, President for the 24 crucial and crisis-ridden years between 1864 and 1888. Brand accepted British dominance on the subcontinent but stoically resisted moves, principally by Lord Carnarvon, the Colonial Secretary, to bring about a confederation of southern African states. However, the discovery of diamond-fields in the northern Cape in 1867 brought prosperity and political muscle, both of which were reinforced with the arrival of the railway in 1888 and the customs agreement with the Cape a year later.

■ The Transvaal's constitutional course was similar, though from the very beginning its settlers tended to be less tractable, more hostile to British influence than those of the Orange Free State. Many of the Boer intransigents, for instance, crossed the Vaal into the northern bastion after the Battle of Boomplaats in 1848.

Independence was conferred on the Transvaal, or more correctly the South African Republic, at the Sand River Convention of 1852. Four years later, despite religious controversy and a great deal of quarrelsome rivalry among the local leaders (much of the territory had been carved up into mini-republics), the State finally managed to elect its first president, Marthinus Pretorius, and adopt a formal constitution. Significantly, it was officially declared that the people of the South African Republic 'desire to permit no equality between Coloured people and the white inhabitants, either in Church or State'. The attractive little town of Pretoria, set in the beautiful rolling countryside of the Highveld and named after the hero of Blood River, became the capital.

During the confederation issue of the late 1870s the Transvaal, predictably, proved the most isolationist of the four white communities, a fact which may have contributed to its formal annexation by British troops under the Natal Secretary for Native Affairs, Sir Theophilus Shepstone, in 1877 (the official reason given for the occupation was fear of open conflict between Zulu and Transvaler – a reason which became invalid after the Zulu empire was finally crushed at Ulundi in 1879). On 16 December 1880 the Boer leaders, who now included one Paul Kruger, reproclaimed their republic, and went to war. Three months later, on the bloody slopes of Majuba Hill, their forces inflicted the first and only defeat suffered by Britain during the whole of Queen Victoria's long reign. Shortly afterwards, at the Convention of Pretoria, the right to internal self-government was restored to the South African Republic.

Majuba marked one more step on the road to the collapse of Boer-Briton accommodation in southern Africa. For the British, it meant humiliation, and a determination in the corridors of Imperial power to salvage national prestige and pride. For the Boers, it was positive affirmation of their strength as a united people and of their ability to preserve their independence come what may.

■ The Cape, meanwhile, had been progressing as steadily if more sedately towards constitutional maturity.

By the end of the century the eastern and north-eastern borders had stabilized: the former with the establishment of the port of East London and the development of small inland settlements, most starting life as garrisons (King William's Town was one of the more important). The frontiers were finally and formally fixed with the annexation of Pondoland (now part of Transkei) adjoining Natal and, in 1895, of British Bechuanaland (now Botswana), a huge northern wilderness area sprawling between the Transvaal and the Namibia of today. The mountain fortress of Basutoland, which was eventually to become the kingdom of Lesotho, had fallen under the Cape administration in 1871 before reverting to direct British control in 1884.

For 40 years after the First British Occupation the Cape Colony had been ruled, autocratically, by a Whitehall-appointed Governor. In 1834, however, a small concession was made to the democratic process with the appearance of a nominated Legislative Council which included five white colonials. Twenty years later, in 1854, came representative government: a Parliament containing a majority of elected members, but without executive control, which still resided in the office of Governor. This final authority was granted the colonists with the establishments in 1872 of responsible government modelled on the Westminster system, and the institution of a fully elected Parliament with virtually complete powers to conduct the colony's internal affairs. The Imperial voice was henceforth to be heard, chiefly in matters of foreign policy, through an appointed High Commissioner. Qualifications for the franchise were on the basis of income and property rather than colour.

■ The second of nineteenth-century southern Africa's self-governing colonies, Natal, had been annexed to the Cape after the demise of the Boer Republic of Natalia in 1844, but became a separate entity, administered by a Lieutenant-Governor, the following year. Towards the end of the decade large-scale immigration schemes stimulated rapid growth during the second half of the century. In 1856 there were about 8 000 white settlers in Durban and its lush hinterland (still teeming with wild game: elephants were foraging close to the city well into the twentieth century). By 1893 the figure had risen to 50 000, with Durban shortly to become one of the biggest and busiest ports south of the equator.

Throughout the century, though, and to the present day, the non-white population was in an overwhelming majority. The bulk of this was the Nguni, predominantly the Zulus, who, despite strenuous official efforts to safeguard 'native' land rights, were provoked by white encroachment to the point of open conflict. The Zulu wars culminated in 1879 with the annihilation of a British army at Isandlwana, the heroic sideshow at Rorke's Drift shortly afterwards and the final and decisive defeat of Cetshwayo's regiments at Ulundi. Zululand was ruthlessly balkanized, divided into 13 separate chieftaincies and then, in 1887, annexed to Britain before being incorporated into the Colony of Natal four years later.

The last ethnic ingredient of southern Africa's heterogeneous society was added in the years after the arrival of the first indentured labourers from India in1860 (see page 12). They were followed to Natal's newly established sugar plantations by a steady stream of Asian migrants. By the turn of the century they, too, outnumbered the colony's white inhabitants.

Thus by the latter half of the 1800s the subcontinent's kaleidoscopic make-up – a mix of peoples of distinct and different identities bound together by history and by geography but of differing cultures and, perhaps inevitably of conflicting interests – had been established: Briton, Afrikaner and mixed-race in the western Cape;

Xhosa and white in the eastern Cape; Zulu, Asian and Briton in Natal; Boer and black in the two republics, with a horde of *uitlanders* – foreigners – poised to invade the about-to-be-discovered gold-fields on the Witwatersranc in the Transvaal.

DIAMONDS, GOLD AND WAR

The discovery, in 1867, of the fabulous diamond-fields of Griqualand West, north of the Cape Colony, was a watershed event: it marked the metamorphosis of what had until then been regarded by Britain as a strategically placed backwater, in some respects more a troublesome nuisance than an Imperial asset, into a very valuable colonial possession.

Prospectors, diggers, drifters, chancers and a fair sprinkling of honest men converged on the fields from all parts of the globe, though there was a preponderance of Cape Britons among the men who were to demolish the original diamond hill, create Kimberley's Big Hole and exploit the world's richest source of precious stones.

Problems there were aplenty during the first few frenetic years of the diamond rush: fortunes were made (and lost) overnight; men lit their cigars with ten pound notes, and the champagne flowed, but there was a much seamier side to life in the dusty, unkempt settlement of tents, shacks and the odd brick building. Within a very short time the population of Kimberley exceeded that of Cape Town, but its residents enjoyed practically none of the amenities, civic or social, of the older city. Crime was rife, alcohol and gambling the major preoccupations, and political unrest a sporadic and rowdy feature of the early years (typical was a comic-opera effort to create a 'diggers' republic' and the Black Flag Rebellion of 1875). Britain annexed Griqualand West in 1871, ruled directly for nine years and then, in 1880 incorporated the territory into the Cape Colony. By this time Kimberley had settled down into a more humdrum routine, its respectable air of permanence derived largely from the stability brought to the fields by a young financial genius named Cecil John Rhodes.

Rhodes had emigrated from England as a sickly 17-year-old and made his way without too much delay to the boom town. Within ten years he had consolidated the small-claim workings under his giant De Beers umbrella (and later bought out the flamboyant Barney Barnato's almost-as-substantial holdings) and, by the mid-1880s, was in control of the international diamond trade. This provided the platform from which he would launch his meteoric career as a politician and empire-builder. Already his vision, which encompassed no less than an Africa painted Imperial red from Cape to Cairo, had taken shape in his mind.

Of greater political significance was the accidental discovery, in July 1886, of gold in the Transvaal – the world's biggest field – on the Witwatersrand, just 50 kilometres from the Boer capital Pretoria.

Paul Kruger, now President of the South African Republic, viewed the rapid influx of *uitlanders* with a wary eye. His strained treasury desperately needed the revenue from the mines and from the 'concessions' – monopolies – he liberally granted to suppliers of everything from beer to dynamite, but the newcomers threatened to overwhelm his small and jealously independent burgher state by sheer force of numbers. Johannesburg's *uitlanders*, for their part, began to demand the privileges of citizenship, reasonably at first, then vociferously, and finally violently.

By 1895 the confrontation between the restive English-speaking community, led by a group of mining magnates who called themselves the Reform Committee, on the one hand, and an ageing President determined to maintain the Transvaal's Afrikaner identity on the other, had grown to crisis proportions.

Early on Monday 30 December, Dr Leander Starr Jameson and his raiding column of some 700 mounted Rhodesians began their famed but ill-judged ride from the Bechuanaland border towards Pretoria and Johannesburg.

The Jameson Raid was the product of a consipracy which had four major elements: Cecil Rhodes, now Prime Minister of the Cape Colony and determined to bring the gold-rich Transvaal into the Imperial fold; the Committee, representing the *uitlanders*; Dr Jameson, Rhodes's man in the field, an adventurous soul who saw himself as Clive of India reincarnate; and finally the powerful British Colonial Secretary, Joseph Chamberlain, whose complicity was covert but real enough. Of all these, only the bumbling Reform Committee was inspired by a genuine desire to rectify wrongs; the main aim of the others was straightforward territorial conquest.

The plan, which called for precise synchronization between the Raid and a popular uprising in Johannesburg, misfired badly. Jameson and his men were defeated, captured, tried and convicted, but the leaders served only brief jail sentences.

Anglo-Boer relations plummeted to a new low. All Kruger's suspicions – of Britain's perfidy and her designs on his Republic and its gold – seemed to be confirmed. Indeed they were entirely justified during the next two years. Chamberlain and his representative at the Cape, the arch-Imperialist Alfred Milner, were more set than ever on the 'unification of Southern Africa' – a euphemism for bringing the Transvaal within the British sphere, by negotiation if possible, but by force if necessary. In the long, weary months of diplomatic exchange and conference the Boer leadership tried desperately to avoid the final breach, conceding to Milner's demands for *uitlander* rights only to find, again and again, that there were other, harsher, demands to follow. 'There is no way out except reform in the Transvaal or war,' insisted the High Commissioner. Replied Kruger: 'It is our country you want.' And, on 12 October 1899, war it was.

Most people – Britain, the European powers, the United States – expected it to last a few weeks. In fact it took over two years for the best of Britain's regiments, almost half a million men altogether, to subdue the rough-and-ready burgher commandos of the Transvaal and Orange Free State.

The Boers had very much the upper hand during the first month or two, notching up resounding victories at Colenso, Stormberg and Magersfontein within the space of a few days, a period that became known to the Imperial forces as 'British Black Week'. They went on to besiege the key garrison towns of Mafeking, Kimberley and Ladysmith; on the eastern flank, the brilliant young general Louis Botha rolled up the railway line deep into Natal. But numbers, and greater resources, were eventually to tell. Redvers Buller finally managed to breach the Tugela line, relieving Ladysmith on 28 February 1900. Lord Roberts and his chief-of-staff Horatio Kitchener pushed through the central front, occupying Johannesburg in May and Pretoria in June of the same year. It all seemed to be over bar the mopping up.

But the war was to drag on for another 23 long months, to cost tens of thousands of lives, and to devastate the northern territories.

Boer commandos under such enterprising leaders as Botha, Christiaan de Wet, Jan Smuts and J.B.M. Hertzog took to the open veld, adopted hit-and-run tactics, and struck repeatedly at the enemy's communications, supplies and outlying garrisons. Against this rapier Kitchener (who was now in command) used the broadsword of blockhouse (over 8 000 of them) and barbed wire, scorched earth and concentration camp. Thirty thousand farmsteads were destroyed, whole villages burnt to the ground. Deneys Reitz, Boer soldier and son of a former Free State president, described a 'driven' area he passed through, 'leaving behind only blackened ruins and trampled fields, so that our course lay through a silent, unpeopled waste, across which we navigated our wagon like a lonely ship at sea'.

The women and children and black labourers of the Boer farming areas were rounded up in their thousands and incarcerated in camps that were designed to intern, not to exterminate. Nevertheless, over 27 000 whites (including 22 000 children) and an unknown number of blacks died, mainly of disease, which spread like bush-fires in the overcrowded, unhygienic conditions. The scorching of the land, and the concentration camps, left a legacy that was to haunt two generations of South Africans.

Finally, the Boers in the field came to terms. On 15 May 1902, at a convention in Vereeniging, their leaders decided to negotiate. On 31 May, after nine days of hard bargaining, the two sides signed the Peace of Vereeniging at Melrose House, Pretoria.

RECONSTRUCTION AND UNION

Curiously, it was the architect of war, Alfred, Lord Milner, who was to become chief engineer of South Africa's post-war recovery. His aims were to repair the ravaged land and resettle the denuded areas; to bring the mines back into operation; to create a customs union, and to consolidate the peace – in fact, to build a new nation. Economic recovery, he believed, would heal the wounds of war, win back the goodwill of Transvaler and Free Stater. He exercised extreme diplomacy in his dealings with bloody but unbowed Afrikanerdom, publicly praising the Boers' 'patriotism, their courage, their resourcefulness, their endurance, their dignity and self-restraint in victory and their stoicism in defeat'.

Behind these splendid and sincere words, though, lurked the old Milner: his brave new world was to be an Anglo-Saxon one. His schemes included the settlement of 10 000 English-speaking farmers on the Highveld 'within a twelve-month'; in government schools 'Dutch should be used to teach English and English everything else', and so on.

His handling of racial issues, too, could hardly be termed progressive. The Native Affairs Commission was almost entirely made up of English-speaking whites, who encouraged the creation of 'locations' for urban blacks and the separation of the races.

Milner's policy of anglicization met strong resistance from the Afrikaners. The recovery programme, on the other hand, succeeded beyond the expectations of even the most optimistic. To help get the economic wheels turning again, Milner gathered around him a group of talented young Oxford graduates – lawyers, administrators, economists: men such as Patrick Duncan (later Governor-General of South Africa); Lionel Curtis, author of the crucial *Selborne Memorandum*; Philip Kerr (who was to become British Ambassador to Washington); Geoffrey Dawson, future editor of the Johannesburg *Star* and of *The Times* of London; and John Buchan (Lord Tweedsmuir), the famed novelist and later Governor-General of Canada. They became known as 'Milner's kindergarten', and contributed brilliantly to the process of reconstruction.

Central to this process were the gold mines which, at the time, were suffering from a critical shortage of labour. African workers, scattered by the winds of war, were slow to return from the outlying regions. Milner decided on indentured Chinese labour, and the first arrived on the Reef in 1904; over 60 000 followed, and the issue became highly controversial both in South Africa and Britain. By 1910 all had been repatriated – but they had served their purpose: the mines began generating wealth from mid-decade on. There was progress, too, in the other sectors: most of the Boers were back on their lands by the end of 1902; a railway line was constructed between Kimberley and the Witwatersrand; another linked the Natal and Orange River Colony systems. A subcontinental customs union came into being in 1903.

Meanwhile there was a great deal of activity on the political front. Het Volk, an Afrikaner organization led by ex-generals Botha and

Smuts, started lobbying for second-language and other sectional rights in 1905. There was also the Oranje Unie Afrikaner party. In due course both groups opened their membership lists to English-speakers; each won a resounding victory in elections to the legislatures of the self-governing colonies of the Transvaal and Orange River, both of which had been constituted in 1907.

Wider concepts, however, were taking hold of men's imaginations: first, political federation; then unification. Jan Smuts summed up the vision: 'What we want,' he said, 'is a supreme national authority to give expression to the national will of South Africa, and the rest is really subordinate.'

Political leaders in three territories and the white electorates of all four were in fact strongly in favour of Union (Natal's politicians were not, but voters in the referendum of 1908 gave an overwhelming mandate to the unionists). A National Convention deliberated the issue between October 1908 and May 1909, and most of its recommendations were incorporated into the Act of Union of 1909. On 31 May of the following year, the four colonies became one country, independent, with Dominion status on the not-too-distant horizon. The form of government – the Westminster system, comprising two parliamentary chambers (the Senate acting in a largely advisory capacity), a cabinet of ten, four provincial authorities with considerable local powers, and a Governor-General representing the Crown – was to remain virtually unchanged until South Africa became a republic in 1961.

Bechuanaland, Basutoland and Swaziland were not part of the new political arrangement. They would remain within the British fold as High Commission territories until attaining full independence in the 1960s.

Significantly, blacks were excluded from the democratic process: they were to be represented by nominated whites. Only the Cape leadership had pushed, and pushed strenuously, for what was called a 'civilization test' (property, income, education) which would enfranchise some blacks and disenfranchise some whites. But the most that liberal-minded men such as W.P. Schreiner, the enlightened Afrikaner François Malan and Premier J.X. Merriman could achieve was reluctant agreement to constitutional entrenchment of the 'coloured vote' in the Cape and the right of mixed-decent people to seek election to the Cape Provincial Council. They received lukewarm support from Natal's traditionally moderate spokesmen and from the British Liberal Ministers, and strong opposition from the powerful northern politicians.

Also significant was the equal status accorded, within the constitution, to the Dutch and English languages. This was a major victory for those Afrikaners who had fought long and hard for all that it represented – Afrikaner identity and the emergence of Afrikanerdom as a coherent national political force.

GROWTH, CHANGE AND POLARIZATION

The years between Union in 1910 and the crucial parliamentary election of 1948 witnessed South Africa's transition from an uneven patchwork of colonial territories to a powerful modern industrial nation. They were also years of war, of profound social change, and of complex political interaction, probably better summarized by broad theme than in chronligical sequence:

The political arena was dominated, throughout the entire span, by three Afrikaners, each of whom had served as a skilled military commander during the Anglo-Boer War.

Louis Botha held the Union premiership until his death in 1919, when the reins passed to Jan Smuts, his close associate and natural successor. Both were statesmen rather than politicians, both believed in conciliation between the two white cultural groups in

South Africa; both were 'Empire men' in the sense that they valued close links with the former colonial power, each leading the country to war against Germany in support of Britain.

The third general, J.B.M. (Barry) Hertzog, was cast in an entirely different mould: a passionate nationalist, determined to entrench Afrikaner power, though towards the end of his political career he was obliged to compromise in the interest of political expediency.

Throughout the tortuous political manoeuvrings of the 1920s and 1930s Smuts and Hertzog occupied centre stage, most of the time in direct opposition to each other but actually coming together in 1933, during the depths of the Great Depression, to form a coalition cabinet with Hertzog as Prime Minister. At the end of the following year their former parties were fused under the umbrella of the United Party and the two leaders directed the affairs of an increasingly prosperous country until the outbreak of the Second World War in September 1939. At this point Hertzog, anti-British to the last, resigned.

Some Afrikaner nationalists, the hardline conservatives, had refused to follow Hertzog's lead in 1934. Instead, they formed their own 'Purified' National Party under the leadership of Cape clergyman and newspaper editor D.F. Malan. Smuts, preoccupied with world events during the war and in the years immediately afterwards, badly underestimated the grass roots appeal – among voters of both language groups – of a movement whose doctrinal cornerstone was apartheid, and at the 1948 general election his United Party paid the price.

The years of war. On two occassions during the twentieth century South African troops took to the battlefield in support of the country's western allies.

Before marching into German South West Africa in 1915, Prime Minister Louis Botha was obliged to quell a full-scale insurrection at home. Memories of the concentration camps and the burning farms were still bitter among many Afrikaners; little more than a decade before, their men had been fighting for survival in their own valleys and veld, and now they were being asked to join 'the enemy' in a wider struggle. Altogether, some 11 000 burghers, led by Christiaan de Wet and other former guerrilla heroes, rose against their government in the traditional Boer 'armed protest'; one large commando, situated near the South West African (now Namibian) border, defected to the Germans.

But the rebels enjoyed too little support in the country as a whole, and the uprising was short-lived: by the beginning of 1915 they had been scattered by disciplined government troops; most of their leaders were arrested and imprisoned; one had drowned in the Vaal River and another was condemned and executed.

Botha could now turn his attention to the real enemy. He personally led a 12 000-man force from Swakopmund, Smuts another from Lüderitz Bay on the western coast; other columns marched in from the Orange River. The terrain was vast, and hostile, but the German-occupied garrison small, and by mid-July it was all over. Observed *The Times* of London: 'To the youngest of the sister nations belongs the glory of the first complete triumph of our arms and the disappearance of Germany from the map of Africa.'

In the long run, though, the new occupation scarcely proved a blessing, certainly not to the international community. Administered by South Africa as a mandate of the League of Nations since 1920, renamed Namibia by the United Nations in 1968, it has been a source of constant diplomatic dispute.

Other South African theatres of operation in the First World War were East Africa and the European Western Front. In both, the Union forces fought with distinction. Smuts, commander-in-chief of the Imperial Army in Africa, executed a long and ultimately successful campaign in the east against the elusive German general

Paul Emil von Lettow-Vorbeck. Bloodier by far were the battles in Flanders' fields. In one, at Delville Wood in July 1916, 121 officers and 3 032 men of the South African Brigade held their positions against massive bombardment and counter-attack for almost a week, the unwounded survivors numbering just five officers and 750 men.

Once again, in 1939, there was controversy over South Africa's obligations. But Jan Smuts – soldier, statesman, scholar, friend of both Winston Churchill and Mohandas Gandhi, member of the Imperial War Cabinet and loyalist (he was one of the prime architects of the Statute of Westminster which, in 1931, proclaimed the Commonwealth of Nations) – carried the parliamentary vote by 80 to 67. Opposition continued throughout the war, its active instrument the underground *Ossewabrandwag*. Generally speaking, though, the opponents of involvement were very much in the minority; whites of both language groups volunteered for active service in large numbers, as did those of mixed decent.

South African troops joined battle with Nazi Germany and its allies, again in East Africa (inflicting a stunning defeat on Mussolini's Italian forces in Abyssinia), in the Western Desert and in Europe, slogging their way up the spine of Italy in one of the hardest and most thankless campaigns of the war.

Economic growth. Exploitation of the Witwatersrand gold-fields triggered the move, from the early years of the twentieth century, towards industrialization, and by definition urbanization – developments that changed the face of South Africa. Primary industry created the base for an impressive superstructure of heavy secondary industries, most notable of the early ones being ISCOR, the massive State-controlled corporation which processes local iron and coal reserves to produce (and export) steel. ISCOR came on stream in 1934. The mining industry has expanded steadily throughout the century, providing a solid base for the increasingly sophisticated manufacturing sector. Two global wars and a world greedy for South Africa's abundant raw materials and processed goods reinforced the impetus.

At the same time periodic drought, depression and new, labour-efficient farming techniques were forcing small farmers and tenant *bywoners* (squatters) off the land and into the cities in droves. The 'poor white' problem was first identified as early as 1890; the Transvaal Indigency Commission reported a few years later that tens of thousands of refugees from the country areas were living 'in wretched shanties on the outskirts of towns', where they competed – largely unsuccessfully – with low-earning black labour being drawn into the industrial system. In 1931 a Carnegie Corporation-funded investigation revealed that, of a white South African population of some 1,8 million, more than 300 000 had to be classed as 'very poor'.

This was of course at the depth of the Great Depression, and things would get better. Large-scale government assistance schemes, increasing prosperity, the organized training skills and the growing manufacturing sector absorbed more and more white labour, and by the end of the 1930s, according to one historian, 'the poor white problem had virtually ceased to exist'. It did, however, leave a painful legacy, especially within official labour policy: the State would borrow from socialism to become the major employer, and job reservation would impose its artificial controls until the 1970s.

South Africa's labour relations story is not an especially happy one. Strikes and unrest were a depressingly regular feature of the industrial scene throughout the decades after Union. Most convulsive was the so-called 'Red Revolt' in 1922. In January of that year 22 000 Rand miners and engineering and power-station workers went on strike and organized themselves into paramilitary

POLITICS AND PROTEST. The years following the National Party's victory at the 1948 polls brought Draconian social regulation, the formal entrenchment of 'apartheid' (later called Separate Development) and a widening racial divide. White liberal opposition, largely English-speaking, became increasingly ineffectual.

British Royalty visited South Africa for the last time in 1947 **(1)**. The new regime **(2)**: Prime Minister D.F. Malan (holding hat) flanked by, from left, C.R. Swart, Minister of Justice for the initial eleven, critical, years of Nationalist rule and who later served as the Republic's first State President; N.C. Havenga, Minister of Finance from 1948 to 1955; J.G. Strijdom, who succeeded Malan as premier; and Dr E.G. Jansen. The personification of South Africa's industrial and financial enterprise: Sir Ernest Oppenheimer **(3)**, whose family has been a powerful force on the side of moderation. Extra-parliamentary political activity in the 1950s included mass rallies by the Torch Commando **(4)**, a movement formed

NATIVE LAWS AMENDMENT BILL
THIS SOUNDS THE DEATH KNELL FOR SOUTH AFRICA UNLESS YOU OPPOSE!

WYSIGINGSWETSONTWERP OP ATURELLEWETGEWING
DIT BETEKEN DIE DOODSKLOK VIR SUID-AFRIKA TENSY U DAARTEEN VERSET!

to protest the new race laws, and silent vigils by the women of the Black Sash (5). Leader of the Parliamentary Opposition during this period was Sir De Villiers Graaf (6), who presided over the slow demise of Smuts's once-mighty United Party. Hendrik Verwoerd (7), doyen of the social engineers and Prime Minister from 1958 until his assassination in September 1966. Nobel Peace Prize-winner Albert Luthuli (8), the non-violent voice of Black aspiration, with visiting US Senator Robert Kennedy. Alan Paton (9), author of *Cry, the Beloved Country.* For almost a century the 'mail boats' (10) provided the physical link and symbolized the traditional loyalties between Britain and South Africa. The last of the great ships, *Windsor Castle,* sailed out of Table Bay on 6 September 1977. The watershed tragedy: burial of the victims of police action at Sharpeville, 1960 (11). Until then, despite mounting criticism, South Africa had been regarded as a full member of the international community; afterwards, the country receded ever further into isolation.

commandos, which were soon enough infiltrated by Marxist activists bent on a workers' revolution. Pitched battle broke out; troops were mobilized; 153 people (including 72 of the State forces) were killed, 534 wounded).

This particular upheaval gave graphic point to one of the constants in the social and economic history of modern South Africa: white fear of black encroachment. Times were hard in the 1920s and '30s; black labour extremely cheap (miners earned 2s 2d a day). It was publicly estimated that if 50 per cent of the white labour force could be replaced by blacks the mines would save £1 million a year (a huge amount in those days). Mine managements knew the facts; so did the unions, and the barricades went up as soon as it was announced, in December 1921, that 2 000 semi-skilled white gold-miners would be declared redundant.

Black urbanization, naturally, ran parallel to white. A new proletariat, officially regarded as 'temporary' and composed in part of tens of thousands of migrants from adjacent territories, collected in the enormous, controlled townships that began to mushroom around the mining and industrial centres of the Reef, Natal and the eastern Cape from the first years of the century. Black security of tenure and the right to collective industrial action were two of the major reforms introduced in the early 1980s.

THE SOCIAL ENGINEERS

The National Party which formed a government – with a slim parliamentary majority of five – under the premiership of Dr D.F. Malan in 1948, remained in power for more than 40 years.

During the first two decades the formal division, or stratification, along racial lines provided the thrust of policy. Separate development (later to be called multi-national development) was seen to be the solution to the immense problems of cultural diversity and conflicting group interests. Linchpin of a Draconian and wide-ranging legislative programme was the Group Areas Act of 1950, which segregated, among other things, the country's residential areas. Further statutes included those involving freedom of movement, identity documents, the formal classification of people according to colour, regulation of workplace and a vast arsenal of security laws.

All this was not entirely new: the ingredients of the southern African melting pot had never really melted. They were kept apart, from the early colonial days, by competition, by perhaps irreconcilable cultural distinctions, by fierce informal pressures and by formal edict. In the words of eminent historian T.R.H. Davenport, the Native (Urban Areas) Act of 1923, for example, 'grew into one of the most complex pieces of control legislation ever devised anywhere' – before the Nationalists took control.

Other precedents abound. But from 1949 there were both qualitative and quantitave differences. Now, for the first time, Afrikanerdom was in the national driving seat, and for the first time rigid segregation was entrenched within an all-embracing legal code and structured administration.

There were laws, too, affecting the coloured people. In 1951 the Separate Registration of Voters Act, designed to remove coloured voters from the common roll (they were to be represented in Parliament by four white Members) was passed but subsequently declared invalid by the Appellate Division of the Supreme Court. Five controversial years later, however, and after a startling series of constitutional acrobatics, the Act became effective. In 1969 the last vestiges of coloured parliamentary representation ended, to be replaced by the partly-elected, partly-nominated Coloured Persons Representative Council (CRC).

But it was the status and future of the black people that preoccupied the Nationalist government. Under Malan and his successors – J.G. Strijdom (1954-1958) and, especially, Hendrik Verwoerd (1958-1966) – the policy of enforced segregation was carried to its logical extremes. In its simplest form, the argument held that the blacks had their own, traditional territories and that it was in these that they should exercise the legitimate rights of citizenship and the vote. The long, laborious process of creating separate black states began in a modest way with the Black Authorities Act of 1951 (it set up tribal, regional and territorial authorities *within* the Union of South Africa), and reached its legislative zenith in 1959 with the Promotion of Black Self-Government Act.

This provided for the establishment of homelands (later known as national states) for the country's main black groups, and for the development in these territories of governmental institutions which would eventually lead, in each case and by predetermined stages, to full independence.

THE REPUBLIC

Significantly, D.F. Malan, just before he assumed office, supported the granting of India of a republican constitution within the Commonwealth. The Nationalists, chafed by the tenuous but irritating Imperial bonds that were the legacy of Union and Dominion status, aspired to the same freedom, and the issue was openly broached by Hendrik Verwoerd in the early months of 1960 (British premier Harold Macmillan's 'wind of change' address to the joint Houses of Parliament in Cape Town reinforced an already strong resolve to cut the ties). A referendum was held later in the year at which the electorate, by a majority of 74 580 votes (1 626 336 were cast), decided in favour of a republican form of government.

In the interim serious unrest had broken out in parts of the country, the culmination of sporadic riots that had started the year before in protest against the enforced carrying of reference books (passes) and largely orchestrated by the Pan-Africanist Congress.

On 21 March 1960 police confronted a large crowd in the township of Sharpeville, near Vereeniging in the Transvaal; shots were fired; 69 blacks were killed and numbers wounded. There were also riots and, soon afterwards, massive protest marches in Cape Town. The PAC and its big brother the African National Congress were banned. A state of emergency was declared.

Sharpeville was a seminal event. Before the shooting the country, for all the criticism levelled at it, was accepted as a member of the international community; after March 1960 it faced increasing isolation. Exactly a year later Verwoerd flew to London to apply for continued Commonwealth membership of a republican South Africa. Harsh words were exchanged at the conference; South Africa withdrew its application, and two months later the Republic was formally established.

Hendrik Verwoerd, Holland-born and Rhodesian-educated, doctrinaire, brilliant, ruthless and uncompromising, died on 6 September 1966 – a victim of an assassin's knife (the killer was a parliamentary messenger, subsequently adjudged unfit to stand trial). Verwoerd had been the chief architect of separate development, designing and constructing a monolithic structure that would become the increasingly sharp focus of critical attention, both nationally and internationally. It would also present his successors with possibly the toughest of political, and moral, challenges.

DIALOGUE AND PROTEST

The man who succeeded Verwoerd, B.J. Vorster, was also a hard-line conservative, but a pragmatic one who perceived the dangerous long-term consequences of isolation and the need to establish 'normal and friendly relations' with African states (in fact Verwoerd had also recognized the realities, but too late to translate conviction into effective action).

The Republic was an African country, the most powerful south of the Sahara; some states were economically dependent on it; the whole complex of southern African nations economically interdependent. This was the era of détente and dialogue, and a significant degree of rapprochement, or at least of contact, was achieved. A flurry of diplomatic activity in the late 1960s and 1970s produced some positive results: Malawi established formal links with Pretoria; closer ties were forged with Lesotho, Botswana and Swaziland; the South African premier paid successful goodwill visits to Malawi (1969), the Ivory Coast (1974) and Liberia (1975). There were reciprocal courtesies: Vorster met Zambia's Kenneth Kaunda at the Victoria Falls in 1975 in a joint effort to solve the thorny problem of Rhodesia's rebellion (the country had unilaterally declared its independence from Britain in November 1965, an act which polarized racial opinion and inhibited the whole détente excercise). In the end it was Vorster who, with Henry Kissinger, the United States Secretary of State, was instrumental in bringing Rhodesian leader Ian Smith to the negotiating table.

Further afield, however, the story was by no means one of unqualified success. On the contrary, South Africa's relations with the international community, with countries beyond her immediate sphere of influence, continued to deteriorate. Criticism of South Africa's internal arrangements mounted at the United Nations; the Carter Administration's Andrew Young stirred the hitherto distracted American liberal conscience; a militarily successful but diplomatically disastrous incursion into Marxist Angola (responsibility was as much Washington's as Pretoria's) helped fix the international spotlight on what was seen as a 'destabilization' policy and on the intractable question of Namibian independence.

Nor was all quiet on the home front. In June 1976 unrest erupted in the sprawling township of Soweto (in fact Soweto is a city of well over a million black residents) near Johannesburg and spread to other centres, continuing in varying degrees of intensity for almost eight months.

The subsequent commission of inquiry found that the immediate cause was the use of Afrikaans as a teaching medium in black high schools. General discrimination, lack of citizenship, restrictions on property ownership and lack of civic facilities were powerful contributory factors. The riots, however, were not spontaneous incidents, but rather part of a sustained, organized campaign, launched by a number of black consciousness organizations, to undermine the social order. In October 1977 the Government banned 17 of these bodies together with many of their leaders.

OPPOSING FORCES

The origin of the South African extra-parliamentary opposition movements – if one discounts the lone voices of late nineteenth-century black intellectuals such as Tiyo Soga and John Tengo Jabavu – are properly to be found in the years of disenchantment that followed the Anglo-Boer War. British 'non-racial justice', anticipated when the two northern territories returned to colonial rule, simply did not materialize, and a number of black congress-type associations made their appearance in the four British colonies (the Vigilance Association in the eastern Cape / Transkei; the SA Native Congress in the western Cape; the Natal Native Congress, and the Transvaal Congress). Such bodies, although vocal, were ineffective.

Nor did blacks have a say in the deliberations that created the Union of South Africa in 1910 (see page 28). Despite strenuous representations to the British constitution-makers, the future was shaped without consultation with blacks. A Durban lawyer, Dr Pixley Seme, became the moving spirit in the launching of the South African Native National Congress in 1912 – a body later (in 1925) renamed the African National Congress.

At about the same time, a talented Indian advocate was crusading successfully for Asian rights in South Africa. Mohandas K. Gandhi had arrived in Durban in 1893 to take up a private legal brief; he founded the Natal Indian Congress a year later and, during two decades of political confrontation (he was imprisoned twice), finally reached an accord with General Jan Smuts. It was during these years that Gandhi evolved his political philosophy and technique, *satyagraha* – commonly termed passive resistance but more literally 'keeping to the truth'. He returned to India in 1914 to work long, hard and ultimately triumphantly for that country's independence.

The history of the black opposition movement – that is to say, of the African National Congress in particular, although labour and church organizations were active and articulate in the between-war years – is a complicated narrative, most neatly encapsulated perhaps by Professor T. Kasis: 'Successively, the ANC retained liberal expectations, became more militant, attempted passive resistance, entered a multiracial popular front, was overtaken by impatient black nationalism, and moved underground.

The passive resistance phase came to an abrupt end with the enactment of the Criminal Law Amendment Bill in 1952. ANC president Chief Albert Luthuli, a Rhodesian-born Zulu aristocrat and churchman, he was formally 'banned' in 1952 but his moral leadership – he advocated universal suffrage but renounced violence – continued to be acknowledged by the majority of members. Luthuli was awarded the Nobel Peace Prize in 1961.

After 1952 the ANC, for a time, operated within a loose, non-racial confederation known as the Congress Alliance whose ideological platform became the Freedom Charter, a code adopted and signed at a rally in Kliptown in 1955. Other signatories were the SA Coloured People's Organisation, various Indian congresses and the white Congress of Democrats.

The Freedom Charter is the key to any understanding of the immensely intricate political scene in the recent history of South Africa. The signatories and their ideological successors subscribed to a non-racial solution to the country's problems. On the other side of a fundamental divide were those who rejected the Charter, seeking an exclusively black, Marxist-socialist solution. This lay at the root of some of the black-on-black violence of the mid-1980s, and it still colours radical thinking within the new democratic dispensation.

The more militant, mainly younger elements of the ANC, those who walked the black-only path, broke away from the parent body in 1959 to form the Pan-Africanist Congress. A year later Sharpeville brought the rivalry into keen focus: each organization campaigned vigorously against the pass laws, urging township blacks to leave their reference (pass) books at home, invite arrest, overload the entire security system.

On 28 March 1960 both the ANC and the PAC were banned in terms of the Unlawful Organisations Act, and went underground, and into exile. The ANC formed its military wing, *Umkonto we Sizwe* ('spear of the nation'): its targets were 'hard' objectives: government installations, communications and so forth. Loss of life was to be avoided. Poqo, *Umkonto we Sizwe's* PAC counterpart, had more murderous intent.

The sabotage campaign was waged until the mid-1960s. There were arrests; some of the leaders, including Oliver Tambo, went into exile; the ANC split once again, the radical communist element departing, leaving Tambo and his nationalists in control. The communist purge, though, was to be short-lived. One of the most influential presences later to emerge on the ANC power base, for instance, was Joe Slovo, a white member of the South African Communist Party (which was banned in 1950) and appointed Minister of Housing in Mandela's government.

Indeed, card-carrying members of the Party filled many key positions in the new democratic administration, though by the early

1990s communism had become a spent force, the ideology discredited, its adherents forced to compromise even on basic principles.

Some leaders, like Mandela, the ANC's president, did not go into exile. At the Rivonia Trial in 1964 he and a number of other Congress figures, including Walter Sisulu and Dennis Goldberg, were charged under the General Law Amendment Act (the 'Sabotage Act') and the Suppression of Communism Act and sentenced to life imprisonment.

The arena, from the late 1960s and especially in the 1970s, became even more crowded. 'Black consciousness' organizations, led by the younger breed, appeared on the scene. In 1977 a full 18 bodies were banned, their leaders detained – including Steve Biko, who died in custody in controversial circumstances.

During the 1980s the African National Congress remained banned. Its titular head, Nelson Mandela, languished on Robben Island and other prisons, and the political arena became increasingly polarized. There appeared to be little common ground for negotiation between the elected government and the disaffected extra-parliamentary opposition; the pressures built up; lawlessness intensified, the violence, which reached its crescendo in mid-decade, falling into two broad categories. First, there was sustained mob unrest – directed at established authority, its sympathizers and at property – designed to 'render the country ungovernable'.

Second, the ANC's campaign of sabotage continued. The organization's operations, however, were inhibited by the Nkomati Accord, signed by South Africa and Mozambique in March 1984; by reciprocal agreements with the governments of Swaziland, Lesotho and Botswana, and by an understanding, based on mutual interest, with Zimbabwe.

A state of emergency covering 36 of South Africa's 260 magisterial districts was declared in 1985, extended shortly afterwards, then lifted in March 1986, only to be reimposed within weeks. This conferred on the Minister of Law and Order and on the Commissioner of Police wide powers to arrest, detain, ban and otherwise regulate to preserve peace and security. The measures had their immediate effect – the incidence of violent unrest declined dramatically – but the emergency cost the country dearly in terms of adverse international publicity, loss of investor confidence and, above all, in terms of political progress.

P.W. BOTHA AND THE PACE OF REFORM

The National Party celebrated its thirtieth year in office in 1978 – three decades during which separation had been sedulously entrenched and which saw South Africa elevated to the higher ranks of industrial nations.

That year, though, was to mark the start of a new era. In September, B.J. Vorster resigned to become State President, and was replaced by former Minister of Defence P.W. Botha. These changes took place in the middle of what became known as the Information Scandal. Probes by press, police and, later, the Erasmus Commission revealed that government funds had been misused by officials in the Department of Information, and that the Prime Minister of the time had known of the irregularities. Vorster resigned the presidency. Also implicated was Dr Connie Mulder, former Minister of Information, who resigned his seat in the house.

The new premier made it clear from the outset that he was determined on a reformist course. The Information controversy delayed the initiative for almost a year, but in August 1979 Botha outlined a 12-point plan to the Natal congress of the National Party: his 'total strategy' for the security and gradual transformation of the social and political order. The plan included provision for power devolution, the recognition of the rights of ethnic groups, the consolidation of national states, the creation of a 'constellation of southern African

states', the removal of 'unnecessary discrimination', and, above all, a new constitutional dispensation (see below).

The most dramatic moves were on the labour front. Two commissions of inquiry, the Wiehahn and the Riekert, had together recommended the maximum use of all available skills and the removal of almost every law that discriminated against black workers. Government accepted most of the recommendations.

Job reservation along racial lines had long been subject to natural erosion, the artificial barriers crumbling under the pressure of market forces. Now, with the active participation of the private sector, blacks were to be brought fully into the body economic through intensified training, integration and the elimination of the wage gap. Collective bargaining, in fact, was to prove one of the keys to genuine advancement. Black trade unions, fully recognized, would be the sharpest instrument in the operation to improve the lot of the urban black. In the event, the unions organized themselves with remarkable speed and expertise, giving the black workforce powerful economic and, potentially, political muscle almost overnight.

In due course, other significant changes occurred in the urban context: black townsfolk achieved a more permanent status with the right to purchase homes on the long (99-year) lease and later, in many instances, to buy houses outright even though they were technically citizens of national states rather than citizens of the Republic of South Africa.

Above all, influx control and the 'pass laws' were finally legislated out of existence in 1986, and a new and far less provocative system of identify documentation introduced.

However, the thrust of the Botha strategy was – had to be – in the constitutional field. The Senate was abolished in 1980, signalling the demise of the Westminster system in South Africa. A new body, the President's Council, comprising 60 nominated coloured, Indian and white members, was established to investigate and recommend a new constitution. This it did, presenting its package in May 1982.

The recommendations, which were accepted, made provision for an Executive President, a Parliament of three Houses (white, Asian and coloured), a non-racial Cabinet; a reconstituted President's Council and changes, intended to accommodate some black political aspirations, at local and regional government level. Prime Minister Botha announced that the proposals would be put to the test of a referendum to be held on 2 November 1983.

Among those who endorsed the proposals were the 'official' Indian bodies, and the Labour Party, for long a major voice of the coloured people and an opponent of established government. The endorsement shattered the credibility of these organizations, dissipating their traditional support.

Ranged against the scheme were parliamentary groups to the left (the Progessive Federal Party, led by Dr F. van Zyl Slabbert) and to the right (notably the Conservative Party). The Conservative Party leader, Dr Andries Treurnicht, had resigned his Cabinet portfolio in 1982, and, together with ex-Ministers Connie Mulder and Ferdinand Hartzenberg, had formed the party to fight what was perceived as a dangerous 'drift to the left'. Sixteen right-wing MPs joined the new organization, whose power-base lay largely in the north of the country.

Strong but voteless voices raised against the proposed tricameral system included those of KwaZulu's Chief Mangosuthu Buthelezi, all the liberation organizations, and the United Democratic Front (UDF), a popular mass-movement formed to campaign, legitimately, for a 'no' response. In the event, the white electorate gave overwhelming approval to the new constitution: 66 per cent voted in favour – a signal victory for P.W. Botha and a rare demonstration of Afrikaans- and English-speaking unity.

The process of reform got under way during the first session of the new Parliament. High points were the abolition of the Mixed

Marriages Act and Section 16 of the Immorality Act. The real significance, though, was that whites and people of colour were for the first time deliberating and legislating together, and that change was very much in the air.

Coincident with all this was a sudden and deep economic recession, triggered originally by unfavourable commodity markets, a falling gold price and State over-spending; latterly by unrest, serious inflation, loss of banking and investor confidence and a decline in the value of the Rand compared with the world's major currencies.

Ironically, or perhaps predictably, this was the time chosen by the black opposition and important sections of the international community to increase pressure on the South African government. The disinvestment debate; sanctions; sporting isolation; township violence and the state of emergency occupied the headlines. Over the months, the reform initiative became subordinate to the perceived need to counter extra-parliamentary opposition to the co-optive approach. By the end of 1986 security rather than political progress was the central issue.

SIGNS OF CHANGE

However, the outlook wasn't entirely gloomy. Even though the hardline Conservatives gained 22 of the parliamentary seats in the 1987 general election and came close to winning a dozen more, it was evident that the ruling National Party harboured a powerful progressive element within its ranks. Left-of-centre independents had also put up a remarkably strong showing at the polls. Clearly, a great many white South Africans did in fact want change.

Moreover, there were shortly to be significant moves towards regional détente. In 1988, under joint US-Soviet pressure, the parties involved in the Angolan-Namibian impasse met in Brazzaville (Congo Republic), Cairo and other venues to negotiate Cuban withdrawal from the subcontinent, Namibian autonomy and a resolution of the Angolan civil war. The Brazzaville Protocol was signed in November of that year and confirmed in New York a month later, setting an April 1989 date for the formal start of the Namibian independence process. In March 1990 Namibia became a fully independent state, taking her place in the community of nations.

Meanwhile, talks had also been held with the Mozambican leadership; the succeeding months saw a marked improvement in relations between South Africa and Angola, and for the first time in a decade there was real hope of an end to the civil wars that had ravaged the former Portuguese territories, and which were bedevilling intra-regional relationships.

These events corresponded with the mood of the times. The wind of change was gusting throughout the world, sweeping away the values, priorities and assumptions of the old international order. The Russian empire was collapsing, bringing down the authoritarian regimes of Eastern Europe, and territorial competition between the major powers had ended. Southern Africa, of course, could not remain immune from the trends.

THE BREAKTHROUGH

In January 1989, President P.W. Botha suffered a mild stroke and, a few weeks later, resigned the leadership of the National Party in favour of Transvaal strongman F.W. de Klerk, who had generally been regarded as one of the more conservative influences in the ruling hierarchy.

Later, after fighting a bitter and somewhat unseemly rearguard action – against senior politicians who were now agreed that the government's anti-communist 'Total Strategy' had become irrelevant, that the era of the 'securocrats' had passed, that apartheid was an anachronism, and that the time had come for an entirely new

dispensation in South Africa – Botha also resigned the State Presidency. The changes that followed were rapid, fundamental, dramatic and far-reaching.

A general election in the latter part of 1989 confirmed that opinion within white society had polarized. The Nationalists lost ground to both the right and to a growing body of realists disenchanted with policies that seemed to be leading only to a nation-wide state of anarchy. Time and circumstance favoured the moderates: pressures to release ANC leader Nelson Mandela, by now the world's best-known political prisoner, and to reach an accommodation with the black majority, had become irresistible.

At the opening session of the new parliament in February 1990, President De Klerk announced the unbanning of the African National Congress, the Pan-Africanist Congress, the South African Communist Party and a number of other proscribed organizations, and the release of political prisoners.

Two weeks later Mandela, incarcerated for the previous 27 years (initially on Robben Island and later in the grounds of Victor Verster prison at Paarl, north of Cape Town), walked to freedom.

The decades of white political supremacy were over; the new South Africa, its shape as yet undefined, had been born.

FIRST STEPS

The journey towards political settlement and the establishment of a fully democratic order within South Africa was long, hard, and fraught with hazard.

The events of 1990, the first year of the new era, set the pattern.

One of De Klerk's first moves as president had been to dismantle P.W. Botha's National Security Management System, a sinister network that had effectively hijacked a large part of the civilian government's authority. This was a major setback for the 'securocrats' – hard-nosed white conservatives, many of whom were believed to lurk in the middle and upper echelons of the police and armed forces and who were determined to sabotage reconciliation by any means, fair or (predominantly) foul, at their disposal.

Much of this covert campaign was allegedly concentrated within the curiously named Civil Co-operation Bureau (CCB), a 'hit squad' which targeted political and human rights activists and which was thought to have arranged the assassinations of, among others, the university academic David Webster and the liberal Namibian lawyer Anton Lubowski.

The Harms commission of inquiry, set up in January 1990, faced bureaucratic obstruction and was obliged to exonerate senior military men and politicians (including Minister of Defence Magnus Malan), but voiced strong suspicions that the CCB was involved in 'more crimes of violence than the evidence shows'.

On 13 September 1990, 26 people were shot and hacked to death and more than 100 injured in the first of many senseless 'train massacres' on the Johannesburg-Soweto line. Reactionary violence – promoted by an undefined but widely rumoured 'third force', and by other groups both to the left and right, each with vested interests in chaos – was to threaten the peace process for four long years.

Nevertheless, there was encouraging progress. June 1990 saw the demise of the hated Separate Amenities Act; and within a year the whole body of apartheid legislation – including the cornerstone Population Registration Act, the Group Areas Act and laws that reserved 83 per cent of the country for whites – disappeared from the statute books.

Things were also moving on the international front. In September of the same year De Klerk travelled to the United States – on the first official visit of a South African government leader in 44 years – to extract a promise that sanctions would be lifted once the reform process was seen as 'irreversible'.

CRACKS IN THE EDIFICE. The two decades since the assassination of prime minister Hendrik Verwoerd (1) in 1966 brought intensifying pressures to bear against South Africa's political and social structures from both within and outside the country. Verwoerd was succeeded by the hard-line but pragmatic B.J. Voster, who in turn relinquished presidential office, in controversial circumstances, to P.W. Botha, a tough, old-style Afrikaner-nationalist forced to make concessions to the changing realities of Africa. Botha's constitutional game-playing divided both his party and the country, handed the liberation movement a whole new arsenal of ammunition and eventually, by default, created the opportunities for true reform. 1976 was a watershed year: on 16 June Soweto students took to the streets to provoke a frenzy of violence and counter-violence (6), the former directed principally at inequalities in education,

6

9

7

8

though the roots of discontent went deeper, nurtured by the apartheid system and its denial of fundamental human and political rights to people of colour. Among the more visible of the system's many ugly faces were the strict segregation of public amenities, including access to public transport (2), and the control of movement through the iniquitous pass laws (4). Recognizing the dangers of international isolation, Vorster, flanked by his all-white cabinet, speaks of the need for regional détente (3). His 'outward looking policy' enjoyed some measure of success, its high point his role in bringing rebel Rhodesian premier Ian Smith (5) to the negotiating table.

Massive anti-apartheid demonstrations in New Zealand (7) disrupted and nearly destroyed the Springbok rugby tour in 1981. More serious were the economic sanctions that were progressively implemented during the 1980s. P.W. Botha launched his reformist campaign in 1984 with the inauguration of the tricameral parliament (8), which gave a limited political voice to the Indian and mixed-descent ('coloured') communities – but continued to exclude the black peoples from the central decision-making process. The official theory, enshrined in the regime's 'Grand Apartheid' strategy, held that South Africa's black majority had its own, historic 'homelands', in which the various tribal 'nations' could eventually enjoy sovereign rights. Ten such homelands were identified, and four were granted full independence.

Widespread township violence again erupted in the mid-1980s (9), leading to the repression of the extra-parliamentary opposition and the imposition of a state of emergency. The odds, however, were stacked against an increasingly embattled ruling nationalist establishment, and it seemed only a matter of time before it succumbed to the forces of democracy.

In December, the European Community began the normalizing process by lifting the voluntary ban on new investments.

The ANC suspended its armed struggle, and on 13 December its president, Oliver Tambo, returned to his native country after an enforced absence of 30 years. Some 20 000 other political exiles were formally granted indemnity.

PAINFUL PROGRESS

Tentative talks between the government, the ANC and other organizations, which had started in 1990, continued through the following year. The leaders of 19 groups came together to inaugurate the Convention for a Democratic South Africa (Codesa) and to sign a keynote declaration of intent to construct a post-apartheid constitution 'by concensus' (effectively, by majority vote within the Convention). Codesa, it was agreed, would have law-making authority and, although the obsolescent three-chamber parliament would retain veto powers, the National Party government undertook to use its parliamentary majority to facilitate new legislation. Notable absentees from the forum, at least initially, were the Pan-Africanist Congress (which continued to take a revolutionary stand) and Zulu Chief Buthelezi's Inkatha Freedom Party.

The issues were complex, some of them seemingly intractable. De Klerk had, from the first, rejected simple majority rule in favour of a power-sharing formula that contained checks against the 'domination of one group by another', a euphamism for entrenching white minority rights. He also advocated federalism – the devolution of power from the centre to the regions. Conversely, the ANC and its partners wanted, among other things, a unitary state and a winner-takes-all electoral arrangement.

Both sides had their trump cards. The government could hold the whole process to ransom simply by stonewalling, and by giving covert support to Inkatha in its campaign for ethnic independence. The ANC, which desperately needed positive results (party rank and file, and the people of the townships, were growing increasingly restive), had immense popular backing and could summon up 'rolling mass action' in support of its demands. It was also prepared to use international sanctions as a bargaining counter.

In the event, the United States Congress, recognizing 'a profound transformation in South Africa', repealed the Comprehensive Anti-Apartheid Act in July 1991. In that year, too, South African athletes rejoined the Olympic movement and, though they performed with only moderate success, their presence at Barcelona a year later helped signal the passing of the wilderness years.

UPS AND DOWNS

Hopes of a political breakthrough were reinforced by the whites-only referendum held on 17 March 1992. The electorate was asked whether it supported 'continuation of the reform process which the State President began on 2 February 1990, and which is aimed at a new constitution through negotiation', and a surprising 68,6 per cent of voters responded favourably. 'Today,' said De Klerk, 'we have closed the book on apartheid.'

But matters suddenly took a turn for the worse. The government delegation at Codesa, basking in the referendum's success and its own perceived position on the moral high ground, over-confident, even arrogant, overplayed its hand, and the talks were suspended.

Other setbacks occurred with depressing regularity, among them:

■ The massacre of 45 innocents in the Transvaal township of Boipatong in June 1992 – a tragedy widely rumoured (but never proven) to be the work of the 'third force'. Evidence gathered by the respected Goldstone commission later revealed a large-scale 'dirty

tricks' campaign sanctioned by senior military officers. A Human Rights Commission report estimated that 3 499 people died in political violence during 1992.

■ The confrontation between ANC marchers and troops of the Ciskei army in September 1992. Thirty of the former were gunned down, more than 200 injured, and the negotiations placed in jeopardy. Mandela and De Klerk, however, moved quickly to defuse the crisis, signing a 'record of understanding' which committed the parties to the creation of a non-racial transitional government followed by the democratic election of a constituent assembly.

■ The assassination by maverick right-wingers, on 10 April 1993, of Chris Hani, general secretary of the South African Communist Party, member of the ANC's inner council and a hero to the young black radicals. Again, the will to make political progress won the day, and the talks proceeded.

■ The continued intransigence of Chief Buthelezi and his Inkatha Freedom Party. The 'Zulu factor' was to prove a serious obstacle to settlement until well past the eleventh hour.

■ Similarly, the obstructionist tactics of white conservatives intent on their own *Volkstaat*, or peoples' republic. The far-right fringe – personified in the portly figure of Eugene Terre'Blanche, leader of the para-military AWB – threatened civil war. The more moderate element, together with the governments of Ciskei and KwaZulu, applied pressure through a loosely constituted body known as the Concerned South Africans Group (Cosag), later renamed the Freedom Alliance.

THE LAST MILE

In December 1993 parliament was effectively superceded by a multi-party Transitional Executive Council (TEC), the product of a negotiation process that had started in earnest two full years before. It convened in terms of an agreement, reached by Codesa's successor in June 1993, on an interim constitution, on the reincorporation of the 'homelands', and on a date for national elections.

The polls, scheduled for the following April, were to be held on the basis of universal adult suffrage, proportional representation within a system of party and regional lists, and the electorate would choose a central government and nine regional governments.

In September Nelson Mandela had called for the lifting of all remaining international sanctions.

Two months later he and De Klerk shared the 1993 Nobel Peace Prize: the two stood on opposite sides of the racial divide, but they held each other in respect, if not affection, and together they had piloted the ship of state to safe harbour.

The last of the obstacles to settlement quickly and, it seemed, miraculously evaporated. A few days prior to the election, in a startling turn-around, Buthelezi finally abandoned his demands for postponement and greater autonomy for the provinces, and agreed to participate in the polls.

After a protracted election process, which proved a lively, often chaotic but always – astonishingly in view of past antagonisms – good-humoured affair, the ANC gained a two-thirds majority in the new National Assembly.

It also captured healthy majorities in six of the nine regional parliaments, shared the honours in the seventh, lost the Western Cape to the National Party (the conservative coloured vote proved decisive) and KwaZulu-Natal to the Inkatha Freedom Party.

Early in May 1994, Nelson Mandela was sworn in as the first president of a liberated, fully democratic South Africa.

SOUTH AFRICA TODAY

South Africa is a region that has seen rapid and fundamental change. Within the space of four years – from 1990 to 1994 – the country negotiated a hazardous and sometimes painful transition from autocratic white minority rule to full democracy. Its political and, to a lesser degree, its economic institutions have been restructured, its society transformed.

GOVERNMENT

The constitution agreed by the multi-party forum in 1993 is an interim arrangement: the present parliament, sitting as a constituent assembly, has until mid-1996 to produce the final formula.

However, its capacity to innovate, to make radical changes to the existing arrangement, is severely restricted by more than 30 entrenched and inviolable principles.

Principal ingredients of the interim constitution are an executive president, a bicameral parliament of National Assembly and Senate, nine provincial parliaments (technically, legislative assemblies) and a Bill of Rights. To elaborate:

■ The constitution is the supreme law. Statutes enacted by parliament must be in accordance with the constitution, some of whose clauses restrict parliamentary discretion – for instance, in matters affecting the Bill of Rights and the powers of the provinces.
■ The National Assembly comprises 400 members elected through a system of proportional representation: the number of seats held by each party is calculated according to the total (countrywide) votes it receives in a general election. Of the 400 members, 200 are elected on a national list and 200 on provincial lists.

In a radical departure from the Westminster tradition, the system makes no provision for members to represent specific constituencies (though they may be allocated to such constituencies by their party leaders). Nor, in practice, can a member vote independently in parliament: his seat belongs to his political grouping, so he is effectively obliged to adhere strictly to the party line. These two elements are seen as major flaws in the interim constitution.
■ The 90-member Senate (upper house of parliament) consists of 10 senators from each province. They too are nominated in proportion to provincial party support. The Senate acts as a watchdog body: it reviews (and may introduce) legislation, though it has no authority to veto decisions of the National Assembly except in matters relating to the powers, functions and boundaries of the provinces.
■ The executive authority has three integrated components, namely the president, his deputy (or vice) presidents, and the cabinet.
■ The president is the head of state and of the cabinet, and 'leads the country in the interest of national unity in accordance with the constitution and the law'. He is elected by the National Assembly.

Provision is made for at least two deputy presidents. Each party that holds 20 per cent or more of the National Assembly seats can appoint a deputy president – a right currently held by the African National Congress and the National Party which, in 1994, respectively appointed Thabo Mbeki and F.W. de Klerk to the office.

The cabinet consists of the president, the deputy presidents and up to 27 ministers. Parties with 20 or more seats in the National Assembly are entitled to a proportionate number of cabinet portfolios. Decision-making tends to be by concensus 'in accordance with the spirit … of national unity'.
■ Regional government: each of the nine provinces has its own legislature, or parliament, of between 30 and 100 members (the exact number depends on population size) and an executive council (cabinet) comprising the provincial premier and 10 ministers.

Again, parties are represented at cabinet level in proportion to the number of seats held in the legislature, and decisions are taken by concensus.

The legislature may devise the provincial constitution provided that two-thirds of its members are in agreement and that it does not conflict with the national constitution.

The provincial parliament has extensive though not automatic powers (there must be proven administrative capacity, and authority is conferred by the central government). Among its functional areas are agriculture, cultural affairs, schooling (but not university education), health, housing, welfare, local government, police, the environment, conservation, tourism, sport and recreation, gambling, roads, transport, airports, traditional authorities and customary law, regional planning and development.
■ Bill of Rights. The interim constitution makes provision for a Charter of Fundamental Rights which safeguards the ordinary citizen from unjust action by the State and, in certain cases, by other individuals. In doing so, it also protects the rights of communities and cultural groups. Every person has the right to, among other things, life, equality in law, freedom from discrimination, security (detention without trial is specifically prohibited), freedom to own property, freedom of conscience, opinion, religion, language, custom, association, speech and peaceful protest; the right to basic education, to a healthy environment, to fair labour practices, and to a secret vote.
■ The Constitutional Court, six of whose 11 members are appointed by the independent (non-political) Judicial Services Commission, is the final authority on all matters relating to the interpretation, protection and enforcement of the constitution. The court sits in Johannesburg.

Foreign policy. South Africa, after long years in the wilderness, is once again a participating member of the United Nations, and has joined, among other world and regional bodies, the Commonwealth of Nations and the Organisation of African Unity (OAU).

Until fairly recently the country belonged in the Western camp of nations, generally supporting United States stances on international issues, though an increasingly hostile US Congress and a less aggressive Kremlin approach to regional conflicts combined to create a major shift in foreign policy – towards genuine neutrality – during the later 1980s. That neutrality (for instance, in regard to the Arab-Israeli and US-Cuba standoffs) has tended to consolidate under the new democratic administration in Pretoria.

South Africa is a minor player on the world stage. But in Africa, the Republic has a pre-eminent standing and a crucial role to fulfill. It enjoys the status of a regional superpower. It covers just three per cent of the continent's surface and is home to a bare five per cent of its population, yet it accounts for:

- 40 per cent of Africa's industrial output;
- 25 per cent of gross continental product;
- 64 per cent of electricity generated;
- 45 per cent of mineral production;
- 40 per cent (in normal years) of maize production;
- 66 per cent of steel production.
- South Africans drive 46 per cent of Africa's motor vehicles and use 36 per cent of its telephones.

The smaller states within the southern subcontinent rely heavily on and co-operate closely with South Africa. The Rand monetary area encompasses Namibia and the independent kingdoms of Swaziland and Lesotho; the Customs Union includes the foregoing plus Botswana. The economies of Zimbabwe and Zambia are largely dependent on South Africa's communications network and its seaports. With the normalization of external relations and the decline of big-power aid, collective enterprises such as the Southern African Development Community (SADC) are vital to regional prosperity – and the impetus within them can come only from South Africa. Nor are such enterprises confined to the economic sphere: already there is talk of a Southern African bill of rights and of protocols for conflict resolution.

And co-operation extends much farther afield. For instance, even during the sanctions era, when contact with the apartheid regime was a cloak-and-dagger affair of covert communication and clandestine agreements, cross-border rail deals were netting South Africa R800 million a year – an impressive enough figure, but modest in relation to the potential.

In 1994, the first year of the new era, Kenya signed a R40-million lease contract for locomotives and, according to reports, South Africa's Transnet utility had agreed to survey Sudan's rail system, and to supply that country with a fleet of 100 giant tankers to ferry in essential crude-oil imports. Large-scale Transnet projects had also been completed or were in progress in Angola, Mozambique and Malawi, and new ones were being discussed with authorities in Zaïre, the Congo Republic, Tanzania and Ivory Coast. Talks were also said to be underway for a multi-million dollar contract with Libya.

Similarly, South Africa's Eskom envisages harnessing the southern region's immense hydro-electric power potential to provide, through an international grid, cheap electricity to countries as far north as the equator. Eventually the scheme could link the generating resources of the Kunene and Zaïre (Congo) rivers in the west with lakes Victoria and Malawi, and the Zambezi River (already straddled by the giant Cahora Bassa dam) in the centre and west.

And so on: the regions of Africa have shared interests and they are drawing closer together – under southern leadership.

All this has its wider implications. In Europe and America, South Africa is seen as the best hope for a continent ravaged by poverty, disease, famine and, all too often, civil upheaval. The industrial world has poured billions of dollars into various forms of disaster relief – unrecoverable funds that could have been far better spent on economic development, long-term health care and the provision of badly needed infrastructure.

United States policy towards Africa, unstructured and even opportunistic in the past, now seems to be taking on a definite shape, best described perhaps by the phrase 'preventive diplomacy'. A great deal more could have been done, so the thinking goes, to pre-empt the indescribable horrors of Rwanda, civil war in Angola, disintegration in Somalia, famine in Ethiopia, had more analytical forethought been devoted to the ominous trends, and the crises nipped in the bud. Preventive diplomacy involves more than just stockpiling food and blankets against the evil day. It calls for a partnership between the United States, together with the other G7 nations, with an enlightened, comparatively powerful regional leadership. South Africa is well placed to assume the part.

Soon after Nelson Mandela's presidential inauguration he told delegates at the OAU summit that Africa would simply have to take responsibility for its own problems and, although he seemed (understandably) reluctant to be drawn too quickly and deeply into the minefield of regional politics, Washington applauded his sentiment. Mandela has enormous stature in the eyes of the world and his personal charisma, his unchallenged moral authority, places him in the vanguard of the continental rescue operation. If his own democracy can overcome its teething problems to realize its huge promise, Africa may yet travel the high road into the future.

Defence. Despite international sanctions – or rather, largely because of them – South Africa has managed to maintain a well-equipped, powerful defence force – one of the biggest and certainly the most formidable in Africa. Local weapons and equipment manufacture, co-ordinated by the government-owned Armscor organization, has filled most of the gaps created by mandatory military embargoes. The degree of technical sophistication, achieved in a relatively short time, has been impressive by any standards. From South African production lines came a large range of military vehicles designed to suit local conditions (the Ratel infantry combat carrier and the various mine-proof trucks are noteworthy); new weapons systems (including the R4 rifle; the SS-77 multi-purpose machine-gun; the high-precision G5 155 mm field gun and its mobile version, the G6); tanks (the Olifant); over 200 different types of ammunition; communications systems (the advanced frequency-tapping two-way radio); Impala and Cheetah (adapted Mirage 111s) jet aircraft and a combat helicopter, the Alpha, for the Air Force; mobile strike-craft, armed with guided missiles, for the Navy. Most of the South African Defence Force's combat experience was gained in the Namibian border area. These operations at one time included a military presence in southern Angola; in fact, at one stage in the late 1970s, SADF columns fought their way to within a few kilometres of the capital, Luanda, but pulled back under intense diplomatic pressure. Their enemy was, until 1988, the South West African People's Organisation (SWAPO). Elsewhere, in search of other enemies (notably the military wing of the African National Congress), they mounted pre-emptive and 'hot-pursuit' incursions into neighbouring black territories.

Priorities in terms of security have changed dramatically since the peace initiatives in the early 1990s, and the need for a large military establishment, and for well-stocked arsenals of conventional weaponry, has diminished. Conscription has been phased out: the new South African National Defence Force (SANDF) is manned by a core of experienced regulars, whose principal preoccuption since May 1994 has been the integration of a motley array of military bodies – the Permanent Force of the old regime, the armies of the four formerly 'independent' homelands, and the armed wings of the liberation organizations (the ANC's *Umkhonto we Sizwe* and the PAC's Apla). Senior officers are being promoted from the higher echelons of all these units.

The first serious attempt at integration was the National Peacekeeping Force, formed to help maintain civil order during the run-up to the 1994 elections. It proved a disaster, but lessons were learned and assimilation – and training in conventional warfare – was proceeding apace at the time of writing. Internal security is in the hands of the South African Police Services (SAPS). However, elements of the military have in recent times assisted – very effectively – in the control of township violence.

The police force, like the army, is undergoing fundamental change. Until 1994 it was widely regarded as the coercive arm of a repressive regime, and enjoyed neither the confidence nor the respect of the majority. It is now being retrained – to be apolitical, flexible, and to serve rather than to intimidate. Psychological profiles have been drawn up for the benefit of recruiting and training officers, and civilian ranks are to replace the military structure. There are also moves towards a system of 'community policing' in which officers maintain law and fight crime in consultation with, and with the help of, the ordinary residents of the urban areas.

The legal system. The first settlers at the Cape brought the laws of Holland with them: a code evolved from the Germanic laws of western Europe, many of which in turn originated in the *Corpus Juris Civilis*, the four great books prescribed by the Eastern Roman (Byzantine) Emperor Justinian in the sixth century. Despite the systematic Anglicization of the Cape from the early nineteenth century onwards, a Royal Commission found, in 1857, that 'the Roman-Dutch law forms the great bulk of the law in the Colony'.

Nevertheless, British influence on the legal system has been considerable, particularly in the realms of court procedure, common law precedent, company and mercantile jurisprudence, and in the rules of evidence. During the period from Union in 1910 to liberation in 1994, a huge and complex network of control legislation overlay common law. However, the apartheid statutes have disappeared, and there have been moves to cut down on the amount of minor restriction and red tape, in the administrative as well as the legal fields, to help create an even freer society.

Ultimate authority in constitutional matters is vested in the Constitutional Court (see page 39). There is also a Public Protector, who is nominated by a joint committee of both houses of parliament (the appointment must be approved by a 75 per cent majority), who protects the ordinary citizen from 'administrative misbehaviour'.

In non-constitutional matters, parliament remains supreme. For the rest, the legal structure comprises:

■ The Appellate Division of the Supreme Court, which sits in Bloemfontein (the country's judicial capital). The Appellate Division, highest of the working courts, is composed of the Chief Justice together with as many appeal judges as the State President may determine.
■ The Supreme Court, of which there are provincial divisions, each with a Judge President and State-appointed judges who may be dismissed only by special parliamentary sanction.
■ Other local 'travelling' divisions of the Supreme Court are the Circuit Courts.
■ The British system of judgment by peers – trial by jury – was established by the first Charter of Justice in 1827. It never proved very successful, however (white juries rarely convicted white defendants in cases where race played a part), and was progressively abandoned after the Act of Union in 1910. In 1969, it was formally and completely abolished in favour of a more workable alternative procedure: a single judge or, in serious cases, a judge with two assessors.
■ Lower bodies include magistrates' courts (of which there are more than 300) which handle the great bulk of routine and minor litigation. Magistrates are public servants appointed by the Minister of Justice, and they perform administrative as well as judicial duties. Many of the more complex and serious cases are heard in the Regional Magistrates' Courts. Public dissatisfaction with the magisterial system is likely to lead to a degree of reform.

■ There are also separate Childrens' Courts, Maintenance Courts, and less formal special courts which give judgment in disputes according to indigenous custom. These are presided over by a chief or headman; appeals against decisions may be made to a Commissioner's Court. A Commissioner has the status of a magistrate but is invariably an expert in traditional black jurisprudence.

Less than three per cent of persons accused of criminal wrong had, until recently, been represented in court, largely because of the sheer volume of 'routine' cases – those involving, for instance, identity documents (it is estimated that some 18 million people were arrested for pass law offences between 1916 and 1985). Even with the demise of apartheid and the extension of legal aid, litigation – and representation in less serious cases – remains beyond the means of the great majority of the country's citizens.

The judicial process, in practice, is generally ackowledged to be slow, cumbersome, costly and, in many respects, ill suited to the new South Africa. Proposals for more expeditious (and better informed) grassroots community tribunals have been debated, but there is deep concern that they would soon degenerate into 'kangaroo' courts. Nevertheless there is a real awareness, both within and outside the legal profession, that some basic and far-reaching changes are needed.

THE ECONOMY

South Africa is an uncomfortable mix of First World sophistication and Third World underdevelopment. On the one hand it has immense natural resources, employs advanced technologies and supports complex industrial and commercial structures. On the other, education standards among many of the people are low; there are too few jobs and services for the rapidly expanding population and the 'poverty cycle', if not as horrific as it is in some other African countries, does exist, threatening stability and profoundly affecting the process of economic decision-making.

The new leadership, which assumed the reins of power in 1994, is committed to a redistribution of the national assets – a narrowing of the gap between rich and poor. Precisely how this is to be achieved was, at the time of writing, still uncertain, though the first national Budget and the launching of the much-heralded Reconstruction and Development Programme (RDP) gave some clear pointers to official thinking (see page 46).

Economic pointers. The most significant contributions to the Gross Domestic Product are manufacturing industry (about 22 per cent), mining (13 per cent), commerce (11 per cent), the informal sector (9,5 per cent), transport and communications (9,1 per cent), and electricity and water (four per cent). Agriculture, forestry and fishing account for a relatively modest 5,8 per cent. These figures reveal the dramatic transformation from an agrarian-based economy a century ago, before the discovery and exploitation of diamonds and gold, to today's advanced industrialization. For much of the twentieth century mining provided the impetus; after the Second World War there was an impressive growth of manufacturing activity. That sector is now the priority: it is capable of much further expansion (South Africa exports too many raw materials that could be fabricated, turned into semi-manufactured or end products) and of absorbing more job-seekers than all the other economic areas put together. This is the vital consideration.

The economy, as mentioned, suffered a number of serious setbacks in the decade before 1994. South Africa is a trading nation (60 per cent of the GDP is represented by the reciprocal flow of goods and services) and is consequently sensitive to international financial pressures. The flexible exchange rate introduced at the beginning of the 1980s led to rapid short-term growth, but also to a

THE BREAKTHROUGH. Towards the end of 1989 President P.W. Botha was ousted in favour of Frederick Willem de Klerk (**1**), a leading conservative who was nevertheless acutely aware of the winds of change gusting through the world, and who committed himself, from the outset, to helping lead South Africa away from the brink of racial conflagration. Lending moral force to the reform movement were church bodies ranging through the religious spectrum, the most prominent of their leaders a courageous trio (**2**) comprising Dr Beyers Naude, Nobel Peace Prize laureate Archbishop Desmond Tutu and Dr Alan Boesak, head of the World Council of Reformed Churches. Serious obstacles to reform lay both to the left, among doctrinaire activists intent on the overthrow of 'white' institutions, and to the far right. Most vocal of the latter's spokesmen was Eugene Terre'Blanche (**4**), whose paramilitary AWB, displaying trappings reminiscent of Nazi Germany, rejected any concessions to racial reconciliation.

Nevertheless, within months De Klerk had unbanned the African

National Congress (ANC), the South African Communist Party (SACP), the radical Pan-Africanist Congress and some 30 other hitherto proscribed organizations. Soon afterwards Nelson Mandela, the world's best-known political prisoner, walked to freedom after 27 years of incarceration, many of them spent on Robben Island near Cape Town. Flanked by his (later estranged) wife Winnie and party elder Walter Sisulu (3), Mandela acknowledges the adulation of a people who, after 350 years of settler domination, sense that liberty is within their grasp. The road to peace, though, proved long, hard and fraught with hazards. Among the most threatening of the setbacks was the assassination, in March 1993, of Chris Hani, secretary general of the SACP, leading member of the ANC's inner council and a hero to the country's disaffected youth (5). But sound political sense prevailed and the negotiations – conducted for the most part under the auspices of the Convention for a Democratic South Africa (Codesa) – proceeded until a broad-ranging agreement was concluded in the latter part of 1993.

The subsequent general election, held in April 1994, proved a remarkably peaceful affair. It had been widely predicted that forces opposed to the transferance of power to the ANC, notably an aggressive Zulu minority (7), would ensure that the polls were neither free nor fair, but their leader, Chief Buthelezi, agreed to co-operate at the eleventh hour. The ANC won just under two thirds of the popular vote in a massive turnout. Polling booths saw kilometres-long lines of people waiting patiently in the hot autumn sun (6) to exercise their civil rights for the first time in their lives. Among the celebrants were Mandela and Ramaphosa (9), one of the chief architects of the transition accord. Two weeks later Mandela was sworn in as the first president of a liberated, fully democratic South Africa (8).

deterioration in the balance of payments on the capital account. Foreign debt accumulated; the Rand failed to rise above its apparent equilibrium level, and sudden loss of international banking confidence following widespread internal unrest and the famed 'Rubicon speech' – P.W. Botha's unexpectedly conservative reaction to pressures for reform – led, in September 1985, to a brief closure of the Johannesburg Stock Exchange, a moratorium on foreign debt repayments and the re-introduction of the two-tier (financial and commercial Rand) exchange structure.

These developments produced some of the major dilemmas facing the country's policy-makers. On the one hand they placed severe constraints on medium and long-term growth (when a government reschedules its debt, future loans become much more difficult to negotiate with the once-bitten bankers); while on the other, internal pressures demand rapid growth. At present, options are limited despite – or perhaps because of – the urgent need for economic and social upliftment. The RDP requires massive funding, which can only be generated through domestic savings and foreign capital investment. The economic future hinges on whether the decision-makers can create the right climate, one in which investors can anticipate a good return on their money.

Mining. South Africa has the largest known reserves of gold, platinum, high-grade chromium, manganese, vanadium, fluorspar and andalusite in the world, and massive deposits of diamonds, iron-ore, coal, uranium, asbestos, nickel and phosphates – a powerful litany of natural endowment.

Gold production averages some 600 tons a year – about 35 per cent of the world output. South Africa's gold mines are the third largest of the world's suppliers of uranium, a co-product. Gold, however, has taken a beating in recent years: international crises – the kind that have traditionally attracted support for the metal – have failed to lift the price above what, for many of South Africa's mines, is a break-even level, though physical demand and other factors prompted an upward trend in the price in the early 1990s.

Diamonds, discovered in the deep kimberlite pipes of the northern Cape, launched the country's industrial revolution in the 1870s and generated fabulous wealth over the decades that followed. The country is the world's largest producer of gem diamonds – and of the platinum group of metals (palladium, rhodium, iridium and ruthenium as well as platinum itself).

About three-quarters of the earth's reserves of both platinum and chromium are locked into the immense pre-Cambrian strata of South Africa's bushveld complex in the northern part of the country. Among the most important of the minerals is manganese, vital in the production of steel and found in great quantities (about 80 per cent of the world's known reserves) in the Northern Cape.

Finally there is coal, of which South Africa has located deposits amounting to 58 billion tons, and which provides the country with much of its electricity and synthetic petroleum. The 100 mines produce about 175 million tons a year, a figure projected to rise to 330 million tons by the year 2000. A healthy proportion of the output is exported, most of it through the east coast port of Richards Bay and mainly to northern Europe and Japan.

Energy. Despite its limited oil resources, the Republic is a net exporter of energy. Coal, as mentioned above, is the principal source: 60 per cent of coal-mining output is applied to the generation of electricity; 17 per cent to the production of synthetic fuels; six per cent to conversion to coke and tar. Three great oil-from-coal plants have been built: Sasol 1 in the Orange Free State, completed in 1955; Sasol 2 and 3 at Secunda in the eastern Transvaal, the impetus for the latter two coming from the international oil crisis in 1973. Together, these establishments consume 32 million tons of coal a year and represent the world's first and as yet only commercial (albeit subsidized) large-scale synthetic fuel operation. Eventually they and others like them will make South Africa self-sufficient in liquid and gas fuels and a host of other coal-based products.

South Africa's largest electricity supply utility, Eskom, which operates 19 coal-fired, two hydro-electric, two pump-storage, one nuclear and three gas-turbine power stations, provides 97 per cent of electricity consumed (some 140 000 million kilowatts annually). Six new coal-fired power stations came on stream in the mid-1980s, including the largest dry-cooled plant in the world, at Ellisras in the Northern Transvaal.

Mozambique, Botswana and Zimbabwe are reliant on South African electricity. Eskom generates around 60 per cent of all power produced on the continent of Africa, and could comfortably supply enough electricity for the needs of every country south of the Sahara. Eskom's annual turnover is bigger than the gross domestic products of most African states.

Offshore oil and gas fields have been located off the south coast town of Mossel Bay, and the first contracts in terms of Soekor's multi-billion rand exploitation programme were awarded in the early 1990s. The decision to tap these resources was taken, years before, by a regime intent on countering international trade embargoes, but now, with South Africa's readmission to the community of nations, it appears that the whole exercise has cost the country dearly, and needlessly. The budget overrun has been massive, and there have been accusations of gross mismanagement. Nevertheless, the enterprise will continue to be operative because too much money – around R14 billion – has already been invested, and no government can simply write off that kind of investment.

Industry. A large pool of labour, a wealth of natural resources, technological expertise and, not least, economic and perhaps political necessity have led South Africa towards self-reliance in industrial products. Manufacturing industry, as we have noted, contributes almost a quarter of the Gross Domestic Product. The larger sub-sectors include:

■ *Metal industries.* The Iron and Steel Corporation (ISCOR) has three major plants which together produce about six million tons of liquid steel a year, with specialized metal products (for instance carbon and stainless steel, ferro alloys, copper and brass, high-carbon chrome) turned out by a number of smaller mills.

The country's engineering and heavy industrial works manufacture everything from cranes and sugar mills through engines, turbines, machine tools, agricultural equipment, structural steel and cables to specialized industrial machinery and computer products.
■ *Non-metallic mineral products* (largely for the construction industry) were running at an annual value of about R10 000 million in the early 1990s.
■ *Transport and equipment.* There are a number of vehicle manufacturing and assembly plants in the country; most in and around Port Elizabeth, the 'Detroit of South Africa' (though the giant Volkswagen works is located farther up the coast, in the small river-port city of East London).

In the 1980s their combined output was some 400 000 units a year (local content has been pegged at 66 per cent), though the industry suffered grievously during the recessions of the mid-1980s and early 1990s and appears to be especially vulnerable to labour problems. Heavy-duty diesel engines for buses are manufactured near Cape Town; gearboxes in Boksburg in the Transvaal.
■ *Chemicals and pharmaceuticals.* The list of basic industrial chemicals produced in South Africa is long, ranging across the entire spectrum from fertilizers and pesticides through explosives to petroleum products, plastics and paints.

■ *Clothing and textiles.* The industry employs about 6 per cent of the total workforce and, because of its labour intensity, has been earmarked as one of the growth points.

However, the interests of the two subsectors tend to conflict: the textile plants need to be protected from cheap imports (though the barriers will have to come down in terms of the 1993 GATT agreements); the clothing factories require cheaper imports in order to compete in external markets.

■ *Food products, and wine.* Again, practically the entire range is locally processed. Drought seriously affected food production in the early 1990s, but improved exports in a few subsectors (notably fresh-frozen and canned fruits and, especially, wine from the Boland region of the Western Cape), following the lifting of sanctions, went some way towards restoring the balance.

Transport and communications. South Africa's infrastructure is the continent's most developed, which has been an important factor in the general scheme of foreign relations. Many of the countries of the subcontinent depend heavily, even for survival, on the Republic's road and rail network.

■ There are some 190 000 kilometres of roads interlacing the country, 50 000 kilometres of which have been surfaced, together with a further 50 000 kilometres of roadworks within the urban areas. Pride of the system are the National routes, comparable to West Germany's famed autobahns. They are used by almost five million vehicles – but not, relatively speaking, very safely: the road death toll is one of the highest in the world.

■ Railways – 36 000 kilometres of track, of which 20 000 kilometres are electrified – are operated by Spoornet, a division of Transnet, the largest commercial enterprise in the country. Transnet's other divisions run the national airline (SAA), the road transport services, the harbours and the pipelines.

Efficient suburban rail networks service the Pretoria-Witwatersrand and the Durban-Pinetown areas, and the Cape Peninsula. Rolling stock is locally manufactured.

Luxury travel is represented by the renowned Blue Train (two trains, in fact) which for decades has been plying elegantly between Pretoria and Cape Town and whose routes were recently extended – to the Eastern Transvaal and, in something of a tourism breakthrough, to Zimbabwe's Victoria Falls. Transnet plans to introduce high-speed (200 kilometre per hour) inter-city trains.

The railways handle some 700 million passengers and 200 million tons of freight each year.

South African Airways, the national carrier, operates a fleet of Boeing 747 airliners over a network that spans most of the globe. The network is expanding as new landing rights are negotiated. Some two dozen other international carriers offer scheduled flights to and from South Africa. Comprehensive domestic air services, provided by SAA and a number of private airlines, link 50 centres within the country. Pretoria-Johannesburg, Cape Town and Durban have international airports.

Agriculture. South Africa is one of only half a dozen or so of the world's net food-exporting countries – a testament in a sense to the expertise of its farming community and water engineers because the subcontinent's natural land resources are poor. Rainfall is mostly seasonal and invariably – certainly in recent years – unpredictable. The soil is not especially fertile: erosion over the millenia and the leaching of Africa's earth during the wetter periods of the continent's history have impoverished the nutrient content over large areas (only 12 per cent of the surface area is arable).

Despite these built-in drawbacks the country has doubled its agricultural output since 1960, and now exports, in an averagely good year, over R10 billion worth of meat, produce, processed foods and forestry and game products together with impressive quantities of wool and textiles.

The diversity of the country's climatic conditions (see page 7) enables its farmers to grow a wide variety of crops, from the sugar and subtropical fruits of KwaZulu-Natal through the huge maize yields of the summer rainfall areas to the tobacco of the more arid regions; and to rear livestock for beef, pork, dairy products, mutton and wool. A succession of droughts and escalating input costs, however, have placed large sections of the commercial farming community under severe financial strain. The situation in the less developed and generally less well-endowed black rural areas tends to deteriorate more rapidly under adverse conditions and in places has reached critical proportions.

Land is central to the post-apartheid redistribution issue. For decades parliamentary law reserved more than eight-tenths of the country for 'white' occupation, and pressures to reallocate this prized resource is intensifying. Direct expropriation without adequate compensation has been ruled out, but the white farmer will no longer be coddled by the State. Over-generous assistance through the Land Bank and the Agricultural Credit Board is a thing of the past (both have been redirected towards the development sector; established farmers will henceforth have to obtain financing from the commercial banks); a great deal of State land will be made available, and tens of thousands of rural Africans will have access to the more bountiful areas.

The ANC government's agricultural policy is aimed at 'improving support for the neglected small-scale farming sector, promoting household food security rather than national food self-sufficiency, boosting rural employment and ending inequality in South Africa'.

Labour. The entire structure of labour and labour relations in South Africa underwent a radical transformation following the acceptance of recommendations contained in the seminal reports of the Wiehahn and Riekert commissions of inquiry in the late 1970s. These made provision for full freedom of association of all classes of urban worker; the registration of trade unions; participation in a formal collective bargaining process; the right to strike; the establishment of industrial councils and of extensive training programmes; a comprehensive code regulating conditions of work; minimum wages and social benefits.

Against the background of over-restrictive labour control that had been a feature of the South African economy since the early mining days, all this was progress indeed. Black workers were quick to organize and to prove themselves highly skilled in the cut-and-thrust arena of industrial negotiation.

The unions are a powerful force for change. Initially they directed their efforts exclusively to the welfare and material advancement of the workforce but later, in 1985, came together under the umbrella of the Congress of South African Trade Unions (Cosatu).

Cosatu became an increasingly prominent player on the political stage and eventually allied itself with the liberation movement, throwing its considerable weight behind the ANC's election drive in 1994. But within months of the electoral triumph this marriage of convenience threatened to degenerate into a power struggle over the country's economic direction. The unions sought government support, as a kind of post-election dividend, in their demands for higher wages and better working conditions. But the ANC, once largely dependent on labour backing, now had to satisfy a much wider range of interests – including those of employers – in order to create new jobs, to combat inflation, to attract investment, and to pay for its Reconstruction and Development Programme.

At some stage there is likely to be a split in the alliance, perhaps leading to the formation of a breakaway workers' political party.

The informal sector. More than half South Africa's economically active citizens are classed as unemployed or under-employed: years of recession, a Third World-type population explosion and massive migration to the cities have created whole armies of jobless people and a deep socio-economic crisis. As a consequence, the past decade has seen the evolution of a flourishing 'informal economy', a euphamism for a myriad micro-enterprises ranging from backyard industries and one-man craft services through hawking and market trading to shebeens (township pubs) and taxis.

Apart from generating work opportunities and income, these tiny businesses are helping develop much-needed skills and entrepreneurial expertise. No firm financial statistics are available (for sound reasons: the informal economy is not regulated and, for the most part, untaxed), but it is reckoned that as much as 30 per cent of the country's total domestic income is derived from this sector.

The big share-out. Almost half a century of institutionalized apartheid bequeathed, among other depressing legacies, a grossly distorted economy and social services sector: in the early 1990s around 45% of the population existed 'below the minimum levels'; 2,3 million people were in 'urgent need of nutritional support' (a terrifying 72 children were dying of malnutrition and related conditions each day); and the housing shortfall was estimated at over 1,5 million units (and growing by the month as thousands left the countryside for the towns and cities).

The ANC-led government of national unity is determined on upliftment on a massive scale; its ambitious Reconstruction and Development Programme envisages huge investments in:

■ *Education:* Ten years free and compulsory schooling for every child; a pre-school reception for five-year-olds; adult literacy programmes; education for the 'lost generation' of youths who spent much of the troubled pre-liberation era on the streets; subsidized university and technical college training; heavy expenditure on new schools, equipment and textbooks.
■ *Housing:* More than a million new houses within five years; the provision of running water to every household; proper sanitation for a million families; electricity to a million homes, and universal (and affordable) access to telephones. Urban hostels – vast, impersonal township warrens originally designed for migrant workers and for long a source of bitter inter-group conflict – are to be upgraded and converted for family use.
■ *Health:* Free health care for children under six; large-scale investment in district health authorities, hospitals and clinics; the provision of basic nutritional requirements for all; supervised ante-natal care and child delivery for all mothers.
■ *Jobs and social welfare:* An extensive job creation programme; a living wage for all workers; compulsory six-months' paid maternity leave for working mothers; the equalization of pensions.
■ *Cost of living:* The reduction of income tax for those earning less than R48 000 a year; the easing of 'fiscal drag' (or 'bracket creep') within the tax system; the abolition of Value Added Tax on basic foods; price controls on bread.

How all this is to be funded was the subject of often acrimonious debate during the first year of the new administration. The inaugural budget allocated a modest R2,5 billion to the RDP, which went some way towards supporting investor confidence – the programme, whichever way one looks at it, is consumption rather than production related, and so the lower the level of government spending the better the prospects for economic growth.

The signs, then, are that government policy is to be directed towards achieving stability and prosperity by attracting private capital and stimulating export-driven (and labour-intensive) expansion in order to create jobs and to generate revenue-producing wealth. Private enterprise is expected to contribute substantially to the RDP.

Nevertheless, the demands on the exchequer are urgent: direct taxation is already at its highest tolerable levels, and supplementary sources of finance will have to be found, the options ranging from a special 'transition levy' on taxpayers in the higher brackets together with increased indirect taxation (VAT on non-essentials, and perhaps a fuel levy) to a fire-sale of State assets, or privatization.

There is a lot of room, too, for trimming wastage – notably by reducing public sector employment, which in 1994 absorbed a staggering 60 per cent of government expenditure.

Of all these options, privatization holds the most promise. South Africa has a top-heavy public sector and an asset sale could, according to one estimate, yield as much as R500 billion – far more than is required by even the most wide-ranging upliftment programme. President Mandela appeared to have discounted the idea soon after taking office, fearing that all it would do would entrench big-company (that is, white) control of the economy, but this eventuality is by no means certain.

There are some exciting alternative models to draw from: Malaysia, for example, has shown that privatization can be linked to empowerment (of the people) to reduce inequality and at the same time stimulate rapid growth.

THE ARTS, SPORT AND RECREATION

Culturally, and in the realms of leisure, entertainment and sport, South Africa offers as varied and pleasing a fare as any other middle-sized country, and perhaps more so.

Its special prides are the game and nature reserves, and the varied and often spectacular landscapes. For the visitor, there is a great deal to see and do; the tourist industry is well-organized; holidaymakers are able to stay in and to travel round the Republic in comfort and, at rates of exchange prevailing at the time of writing, are able to do so relatively cheaply.

The arts. The scene is lively, and much of it of international standard. Literature, the visual arts, theatre, ballet, opera and symphonic music thrive enthusiastically in South Africa's major centres. Much of the activity falls within the ambit of the four State-sponsored performing arts councils. Together they employ over 2 000 artists and theatre technicians and stage around 300 shows of one sort or another each year in a variety of splendid buildings. Most notable of these are probably the grand Nico Malan theatre complex in Cape Town (opera house, drama theatre, three smaller auditoriums and a full resident orchestra), Pretoria's State Theatre and Bloemfontein's Sand du Plessis Opera House.

Excellent independent (independent of the arts councils, that is) symphony orchestras are based and give regular performances in Durban, Johannesburg and Cape Town. Also among the more outstanding of the non-governmental enterprises are the Baxter Theatre complex near Cape Town's university and the Market Theatre in Johannesburg. Grahamstown, in the Eastern Cape region, hosts the annual Festival of the Arts, which attracts almost 100 000 visitors a day to make it the largest such event in the southern hemisphere.

The lifting of the cultural boycott in 1993 has opened the artistic floodgates, and offerings at the festival – theatre, music, dance and much else – are drawing increasingly from the creativity of other parts of Africa, and from the wider world.

South Africa has produced a number of gifted instrumentalists, opera singers and ballet dancers. The country, though, finds it difficult to retain its own: universities and other learning centres turn out an unusual wealth of young talent which is often lost to the more sophisticated stages and concert halls of Europe and America.

Music of a different kind is emerging from the black community to make its mark beyond the borders of the country.

The African people have ancient traditions, and a natural talent for harmony and spontaneous song. Folk music, in the country areas, still plays a powerful role in ceremony and ritual. Western culture, and especially religious conversion, has modified the forms of expression (or rather, has added new dimensions to it) but the inborn gift of group singing remains untarnished.

And with urbanization, a new and distinct sound has evolved in the townships. Called 'mbaqanga', it stems in part from the original music of Africa, which was exported to America, refined there and returned as jazz which, in turn, has been changed and given a vibrant new character – a hybrid of of many eras, many styles (the 'mbubi' vocal orchestra, lilting 'marabi', penny-whistle 'kwela', Dixieland, big-band, reggae, soul, rock) but with a personality very much its own.

Radio and television services are comparatively extensive – compared, that is to say, with the size of the population. There are four national television channels, including a subscriber (cable) service run by private enterprise. In 1994 there was one English radio service, one Afrikaans, one popular music (Radio Five), and a plethora of regional and African-language stations. A major rationalization of the broadcasting services is under way: programming and language policies are being adjusted better to reflect the country's diversity of cultures, and there is now a more liberal official attitude to the granting of broadcasting licences.

South Africa can claim few literary giants of the kind that one might expect to have emerged in a country of such beauty, complexity, conflict and tragedy. There has been no Steinbeck to give voice to the wrath of the economically underprivileged; no James Baldwin to bring fiery articulation to ethnic consciousness; no Orwell, no Solzhenitsyn. It could, though, be that very complexity that has inhibited the pen.

Says Nadine Gordimer, a leading contemporary novelist: 'Living in a society that has been as deeply and calculatedly compartmentalized as South Africa's has been under the colour bar, the writer's potential has unscalable limitations.'

Nevertheless, there have been and are South African writers of real stature: the much under-estimated Olive Schreiner; the eccentric Roy Campbell; the mystic Eugène Marais, and, of recent vintage, Alan Paton and Laurens van der Post who each, in his own way, has bared the soul of his beloved country; Nadine Gordimer and J.M. Coetzee; André Brink and Etienne Leroux; the brilliant Athol Fugard and his fellow playwright Gibson Kente.

Among the African people there is, too, a powerful tradition of oral literature: the key to their past, and perhaps the door to the country's literary future. This has played its part in what is known as 'black theatre', a unique art form in which productions are conceived, written and performed by black artists largely for black audiences and which are noted for their sparkling spontaneity. Players tend to share in the creation of the work rather than follow a predetermined script; the shows are invariably an exuberant mix of words, music, song and dance, and some of them have been performed to acclaim on the stages of Europe and America. At one time much of the subject matter, especially in the more orthodox dramas, reflected (and protested) the harshness of life under apartheid, but authors are now moving away from localized, race-preoccupied introspection towards more universal themes.

Sport. South Africans are a sport-loving people, the white community almost to the point of fanaticism. Rugby comes close to being an obsession among Afrikaans-speakers, and Springbok sides from the turn of the century to the 1970s were for long periods regarded as unofficial world champions. Cricket comes a close second.

Football reigns supreme within the black community: there are 12 000 soccer clubs and 750 000 soccer players in South Africa.

World-class athletes have emerged (Bruce Fordyce, Matthews Temane, Elana Meyer), as well as great cricketers (Pollock, Barlow, Richards, Proctor, Wessels, Donald); rugby players (too many of them to enumerate); boxers (Brian Mitchell); motorcyclists; golfers (Gary Player, Ernie Els), and tennis stars. But from the early 1980s South Africa became increasingly isolated from the mainstream of international sport, and standards fell across the board.

With the initiation of internal political dialogue in 1990, the steady removal of apartheid structures and progress towards full democracy in 1994, the integration of sport at all levels has proceeded rapidly and the country's sportsmen have now re-entered the world arena – with, to put it kindly, mixed results. Cricket made the first and perhaps most spectacular move back into international competition: the national eleven held its own during a short tour of India in 1991, commendably reached the semi-finals of the World Cup in Australia and New Zealand the following year, came to grief against the highly professional and battle-hardened West Indians in the Caribbean, and then made a fine start to their 1994 tour of England with a stunning victory at Lords. In mid-1992 a South African squad took part in the Barcelona Olympics, and failed to make an impression, though tennis (Wayne Ferreira) and middle-distance running (Elana Meyer) yielded silver. Rugby's re-entry also showed just how severely isolation had affected the game in South Africa: the Springboks were convincingly defeated by New Zealand, Australia, France and, in 1994, again by New Zealand. Football fared no better.

However, the picture should change dramatically within a year or so – once the country's sportsmen have gained experience at international level, and once the immense talent that lies within the black community begins to be discovered, refined and tested.

South Africa is to host the 1995 Rugby World Cup, and Cape Town, the Mother City, stands an excellent chance of being invited to stage the 2004 Olympic Games.

Game parks and nature reserves. The southern Africa environment is under serious threat – from poachers, from urban and industrial development, from domestic cattle and the encroaching farmlands, from the voracious appetite of expanding rural communities for water, firewood, grazing, living room. These are the intractable problems of Africa – indeed of the entire Third World – and they are likely to remain with us for a long time to come. However, the decision-makers recognize the value of eco-tourism, and they are putting a great deal of money and effort into the preservation of the wilderness. In this context, one trend is especially worth noting. There is now a general conviction that the wellbeing of wildlife and the interests of tourism need not be in conflict with the needs of the rural people, and recent years have seen the appearance of what is variously called the 'multi-use', the 'resource' and the 'contractual' area – integrated reserves in which the people of the countryside, instead of being moved away from the conservation project (as they have been, often controversially, in the past), stay where they are and help look after the environment. In return, they are able to share in its resources – and benefit financially from tourism development. It is a win-win approach – everybody gains, nobody loses – and it holds great promise for the future.

South Africa has nearly 20 national parks, about 500 smaller (some very small) reserves run by regional and local authorities, and a growing number of private game properties, many of them catering for the luxury market.

■ Biggest and most famed of the conservation areas is the Kruger National Park in the Lowveld of the north-eastern corner of the country – a long, narrowish 20 000 square-kilometre stretch of bushveld the size of Wales, bounded in the south by the Crocodile River, in the east by Mozambique, in the north by the Limpopo River and in the west by the lovely eastern Transvaal lowlands. Close to its western borders are a dozen and more private reserves.

This is big game country. The Kruger has 137 species of mammal, including the 'big five' – elephant (10 000), lion, leopard, buffalo (30 000), rhino, immense numbers of antelope (including 100 000 impala), 450 species of bird, 114 of reptile, 40 of fish, 33 of amphibian and 227 species of butterfly. There are some two dozen rest-camps – the larger ones virtual villages of comfortable, thatched rondavels clustered around a central complex of restaurants and shops – and 1 880 kilometres of tarred or well-gravelled roads that lead visitors to water-holes, picnic spots and viewing-sites.

For all the magnificence of raw Africa that it encloses, the Kruger National Park is designed for the comfort-conscious family group – the idea being to allow as many South Africans as possible to enjoy their natural heritage. It succeeds admirably in its objective. At peak periods the park accommodates some 5 000 visitors daily.

Other parks and reserves worthy of special mention are:

■ The scenically lovely Golden Gate Highlands National Park. Situated in the Orange Free State some 360 kilometres south of Johannesburg, the park has an attractive variety of wildlife (mainly buck) and is notable for its birds of prey.

■ The Mountain Zebra National Park, located in the Great Karoo region on the northern slopes of the Bankberg range west of Cradock, is haven to this rare, at one time almost extinct, species. Twenty years ago there were just 25 of the animals in existence; today between 200 and 300 roam the sweet-thorn and succulent-covered slopes of the park.

■ The Addo Elephant National Park was established in the 1930s to protect the last of the great herds of the eastern Cape. Situated about 70 kilometres north of Port Elizabeth, its tangled vegetation and low tree-cover sustain a three-fold higher density of elephant population than any other tract of land in Africa, together with black rhino, a variety of antelope and some 170 species of bird.

■ Similarly, the Bontebok National Park in the south-western Cape, close to Swellendam, was launched to rescue the species (its cousin, the bluebuck, became extinct in the early nineteenth century). The original breeding herd numbered just 17 animals; today the bontebok population is well established. Bird life here, too, is prolific: over 180 species have been identified.

■ North of the Addo is the Zuurberg National Park, proclaimed in 1985 to conserve the region's distinctive vegetation types.

■ The Tsitsikamma National Park and its neighbouring Tsitsikamma State Forest sprawl along the southern Cape's attractive Garden Route. The latter was proclaimed in order to preserve the dense, ancient yellowwoods (one spectacular specimen is 37 metres tall and has a 30-metre spread), candlewoods and assegais. Here and in the surrounding area there are something over 30 tree species, a thick undergrowth of ferns and lichens, and some of the country's finest hiking and walking trails. The national park is designed to protect both the marine life and the shoreline of lovely cliffs, river gorges and rich vegetation of yellowwood, fern, orchid, protea and myriad species of lily.

■ Other notable coastal-zone sanctuaries include the recently proclaimed West Coast National Park, centred on Langebaan lagoon, home to some 40 000 wading birds, and the Knysna and Wilderness lake areas in the southern Cape.

■ The Karoo National Park is situated near Beaufort West, some 480 kilometres north-east of Cape Town. The Great Karoo, an arid but hauntingly beautiful region, has a unique dwarf vegetation which the park helps to preserve.

■ North of Kimberley in the Northern Cape is the recently proclaimed Vaalbos National Park, a preserve of camel-thorn, camphor bush and a number of other distinctive floral species.

■ The Kalahari Gemsbok National Park, almost 100 000 hectares in extent, is South Africa's second biggest reserve. A wilderness of red dunes and dry river-beds, sparse grass and thornbush, it lies between Namibia and Botswana. Despite the general lack of water, huge herds of antelope – blue wildebeest, springbok, eland, gemsbok – thrive by supplementing their diet with moisture-bearing plants such as tsamma melon and wild cucumber.

■ The recently created Richtersveld National park, a vast, dry expanse of harsh scrubland, grassy plain and rugged hill in the Namaqualand seaboard region of the Northern Cape bordering the Orange River.

■ The Augrabies Falls National Park lies astride the Orange River west of the lonely town of Upington, and is renowned for its magnificent waterfalls and gorge. The former plunge more than 90 metres, first in a series of steps and then in one final great leap.

■ The Royal Natal National Park – which, despite its name, is controlled by the KwaZulu-Natal parks authorities and not by the national body – lies within the high fastness of the Drakensberg range, its western extremity bordering on Lesotho. Famed more for its scenic splendour and mountaineering (walking as well as climbing) attractions than for its wildlife, it nevertheless offers much to the naturalist: immense forests of yellowwood; wild orchid, aloes, ancient cycads and the brilliance of everlastings. There is a fascinating variety of birdlife, including three of the world's seven species of crane and an impressive number of raptors – jackal buzzard, martial eagle, black eagle and the rare and beautiful lammergeier that makes its home in the highest of the cloud-combed peaks.

■ The KwaZulu-Natal game reserves, run by dedicated teams of scientists and conservationists, are some of the most impressive in Africa. The climate is invariably warm to hot, humid in the lower areas; the terrain is lush, with an astonishing variety of woodland, forest, savanna, thornveld, riverine and grassland plant species.

Hlhluwe Game Reserve, for instance, is just six per cent of the size of the Kruger National Park but harbours 68 per cent of the total number of the Kruger's species. Game – from lion through rhino to a score of antelope species – is prolific.

Apart from Hluhluwe, reserves well worth a visit include Mkuzi, Ndumo (wonderful numbers of tropical birds), Umfolozi (home to the once-threatened white rhino) and the Greater St Lucia Wetland Park. Most scenically spectacular of KwaZulu-Natal's parks is probably the Giant's Castle section of the Drakensberg: it encompasses the 3 207-metre high massif of the Castle itself as well as the lovely forests and sandstone cliffs of the Injasuti Valley.

South Africa's parks and reserves are permanent features of a sub-continent that, in so many other respects, is undergoing the trauma of rapid change. This is an age of transition; society and its institutions are being restructured; the process could be long and painful; the outcome is uncertain. But there is comfort in the knowledge that, whatever else the future holds, the country will still and always have its precious metal heritage, its stunning diversity of scenic splendour, its far horizons.

Study in contrasts. Johannesburg, one of the world's mining and financial capitals, is aggressively modern, vibrant, brash. But for all the surface sophistication there is still something of its rugged digger origins about the place, seen in the random architecture and sensed in the life-styles of its citizens.

1

2

Johannesburg is barely a century old: a hundred years ago the area was a silent, sunlit stretch of near-virgin highveld that sustained a scatter of kraals, the occasional lonely farmstead and very little else. But in 1886 an Australian drifter named George Harrison accidentally stumbled on the world's richest treasure-house of gold beneath the 'ridge of white waters' – the Witwatersrand. Today the city (1) is at the epicentre of one of Africa's greatest conurbations, a bustling, polyglot metropolis surrounded by dense rings of satellite towns which, together, generate some 60 per cent of the country's wealth. Central Johannesburg has lost much of its commercial glitter to the vigorous new suburbs in recent years but there are imaginative plans to restyle the business district.

3

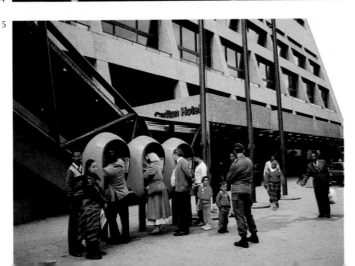

Despite Johannesburg's wealth, and there is a great deal of it, for the majority of Witwatersrand residents life remains a struggle – to make ends meet, to obtain and hold on to a job and a decent place to live; and, as patient commuter queues illustrate (2), to get to and from work on an overloaded public transport system. Nearby is Diagonal Street, home of the Johannesburg Stock Exchange (3), which contrasts sharply with one of the comparatively few remaining city-centre buildings that date back to Johannesburg's infant years (4), a ramshackle home to an Indian family, part of a small but remarkably unified minority. One of the city's focal points is the Carlton Centre (5 & 6), a giant hotel, office and shopping complex. The Centre's obser-vation deck offers commanding views of the city and its surrounds.

Suburban panorama. Modern, upmarket shopping centres are a feature of Johannesburg's suburbia, especially in the wealthier, mainly northern parts. Rosebank, with its imaginative shopping malls and *alfresco* arteries (1) is but one example of the movement of business away from the city centre. Focus of the very affluent Sandton area and arguably the most impressive development of all, however, is Sandton City (2 and 3) with its magnificent hotel, complete with glass-and-gold atrium.

Not all of Johannesburg, though, is brand new: one of the mansions of the early mining magnates (5) is a reminder of a more sedate area, while the entrance to the Great Hall of the University of the Witwatersrand (6) is symbolic of a proud academic heritage. Among Johannesburg's premier tourist attractions is Gold Reef City (7), a splendidly imaginative re-creation of the pioneer mining settlement centred around the old Crown Mines workings (during their lifetime they yielded a fabulous 1,4 million kilograms of gold). Attractions include a Victorian funfair, a replica of the old Theatre Royal and of an early brewery, pub, Chinese laundry, cooperage, newspaper office, printing works, and much else. Johannesburg's affluent northern suburbs (8) are graced by broad, tree-lined avenues, spacious homes, sculptured gardens, and swimming pools.

1

2

3

4

1

Leisure time. Johannesburgers love their sport, as do most South Africans. Among the whites, the national game, perhaps the national obsession, is rugby, and despite virtual exclusion from the international arena the country still manages to produce some of the world's finest players. The new Ellis Park stadium (1 & 3) can accommodate about 90 000 spectators. The ground is also used for soccer, which has an enormous following, especially within the black community – there are 10 000 football clubs and some 600 000 players in South Africa. But horse-racing was the first of Johannesburg's sporting preoccupations, drawing the crowds while diggers' tents still littered the veld. Today gold and the turf still co-exist, but instead of tents a huge mine headgear provides the backdrop to an afternoon at the races (4 & 5). Among the many gentler pursuits are visits to the Zoo (2) and its lake, and to the Santarama miniature city (6), modelled on the famed Madurodam in Holland. Santarama has a scale 1:25, and its patrons are charmed by the splendid musical fountain.

2

1

2

3

4

Every South African urban complex has its high-density black townships. In the early days they were called 'locations', and until quite recently their people were, for the most part, classed as 'temporary' residents and deemed to belong in traditional 'homelands'. That is all changing, though the transition brings its own discomforts. Blacks may now own houses under long-lease or freehold title; the whole thorny issue of influx control – an unsuccessful and painful attempt to halt urban drift – is subject to radical revision; there is a move towards general de-regulation and the encouragement of an informal economy (cottage and backyard industry). Soweto (1-7) is by far the largest of South Africa's black townships, officially accommodating a little over a million people, unofficially perhaps twice that number. Sprawling, grimy, dreary for the most part, it does have its better houses, paved roads, street lighting; its shops, pubs, shebeens and an animation all its own.

South Africa has produced nearly half the world's gold over the past decades, and is currently responsible for 60 per cent of the free world's output. Other metals and minerals contribute substantially to the national wealth: 59 in all are mined or quarried, including large and strategically valuable quantities of manganese, platinum and chromium (of which South Africa has the largest of the earth's known deposits); diamonds, coal, uranium, asbestos, nickel and phosphates.

1

2

3

Gold mining is for the most part labour-intensive, with the majority of workers coming as migrants from national states within the borders of South Africa: for example, the Transkei, Ciskei, KwaZulu and Bophuthatswana. They also come from Mozambique, Botswana, Lesotho, Swaziland and Malawi – and are important foreign exchange earners for these countries. Among the biggest and deepest mines in the world are those near Carletonville on the Far West Rand – at Western Deep Levels, for example, gold is being won 3 780 metres below the surface.

4

5

Nearby, the huge operations at East and West Driefontein provide a glimpse of a day on the mines: learning to lay tracks at the mine's training school (1), drilling deep underground (3), pouring the molten metal (4), cleaning ingots (5) and coming off shift (6 & 8) at the end of a tough but comparatively well-paid day to a meal in the canteen (2). On most mines, sporting and recreational facilities are excellent, while pursuits such as traditional dancing (7) are also popular.

Seat of government. South Africa has three capitals: Cape Town (legislative); Bloemfontein (judicial); and Pretoria, the country's administrative headquarters, a city that nestles comfortably among the eastern foothills of the Magaliesberg. Some 60 kilometres north of frenetic Johannesburg, Pretoria is a quiet, well laid out, dignified town of jacaranda-lined streets, neat gardens, public parks (over 100 of them), monuments and some fine buildings, two of the more notable being the neo-classical Palace of Justice (1), and the Union Buildings (5 & 6), which preside over the city from Meintjeskop, highest of the surrounding hills. Designed by the renowned architect Herbert Baker, the Union Buildings were completed in 1913 and served as a model for the grander but no more attractive Raj legislature in New Delhi. Atop another of Pretoria's hills is the imposing University of South Africa (4), a non-residential institution with a huge enrolment. Tuition is entirely by correspondence. Despite its slower pace, however, the city is not without its bustle of traffic, pedestrians and shopping centres (2, 3, 7 & 8).

5

6

7

8

Jacaranda city. Pretoria is famed for its 50 000-plus, vividly colourful jacaranda trees (1), the first two of which were imported from Rio de Janeiro in 1888. Just outside the city on yet another hilltop is the Voortrekker Monument (2 & 3), started in 1938 and completed in 1949 to commemorate the pioneers of the Great Trek. It comprises a cenotaph, lower hall and Hall of Heroes, whose interior walls display an impressive 92-metre-long frieze depicting the main events of the Trek.

The Treaty of Vereeniging, which brought to an end the long, bloody and mutually exhausting war between Boer and Briton, was signed on 31 May, 1902 in Pretoria's gracious Melrose House (6), Lord Kitchener's residence at the time, later High Commissioner Lord Milner's and now a beautifully preserved showpiece. Focal point of the Transvaal's performing arts is the State Theatre (4) – modern, luxuriously appointed and equipped.

Pretoria's Fountains Valley Park (5), complete with miniature railway (7), is a popular venue for a family braai – the barbecue is a national institution, but the convenience of a gas cooker is making inroads on the traditional wood-coal fire.

Northern playground. Legal restrictions on gambling in many of the former national states – the ethnic 'homelands' created by the apartheid regime – were minimal, and imaginative entrepreneurs took full advantage of tourism opportunities. Glittering hotels and casinos now play host to tens of thousands of South Africans as well as to visitors from abroad. Most popular of the resorts is Sun City, an enormous and gleefully materialistic concrete-and-tinsel complex that offers superb hotel accommodation (1), roulette, blackjack and the ubiquitous one-armed bandit; imported

big-name entertainers, wining, dining, lavish caberet and *risque* films; world title fights, golf, watersports (3) and poolside relaxation on an island of green grass, palm trees and crystal clear fountains; all of which contrasts sharply with the surrounding dry, dusty thornveld.

Latest addition to the complex is the magnificent Lost City development (2 and 4), whose centrepiece is the elaborately domed and minareted Palace Hotel. Hospitality king Sol Kersner has described The Palace and its lavishly landscaped grounds (they have, among much else, their own 'instant' jungle of 4 000 trees that range through the species spectrum) as 'a fantasy come to life … steeped in the grandeur of old Africa'.

Sun City is a comfortable one-and-a-half-hour drive from Pretoria and Johannesburg. Most of the hotel-casino developments are oases of luxury, and valuable revenue-earners, in otherwise poverty-stricken regions.

4

The northern parts of the Transvaal are farmlands and flattish bushveld, dominated by massive baobab and mopane trees and stretching to distant hills, most spectacular of which are the Soutpansberg, a 130-kilometre range that divides the northern Lowveld from the high country to the southeast, and whose summit is a fertile, cool plateau settled by the southward-migrating Venda people in the early 18th century. The region is also home to other tribal and national groups, including the North-Sotho and Ndebele. Venda is in fact a national state, albeit a miniscule one of just 6 000 square kilometres and a population of fewer than half a million, 50 000 of whom earn their living (and provide much of Venda's national income) as migrant workers in South Africa.

A rural miscellany. Venda women at their riverside chores (**1**). A North-Sotho farm labourer, her child safe and asleep on her back (**2**). Part of the Honnet Nature Reserve (**3**), between the Soutpansberg and the Limpopo River. Sunflowers (**4**), one of the area's most profitable commercial crops and a valuable source of vegetable oil. Sotho baskets for sale at a roadside (**6**). An Ndebele kraal (**5**) and Ndebele girls (**7**) in traditional dress.

5

6

7

2

1

3

5

4

The edge of the Escarpment. A waterfall plunges down from the 2 127-metre high Wolkberg (1) at the head of the Magoebaskloof, one of the loveliest, most fertile parts of the country. An especially fine scenic drive is the 97-kilometre road that leads through these spectacular hills and valleys from Pietersburg to Tzaneen, dropping 600 metres in one six-kilometre stretch of thick, dark-green woodland. Sawmills are a feature of the area and although timber plantations abound – such as the one around the Magoebaskloof Dam (2) – the upper slopes are graced by glades of indigenous trees: red stinkwood, ironwood, yellowwood, cabbage tree and the superb 'rooihout' *(Ochna o'connorii)*. Above the dam is the Debegeni waterfall (5), the name meaning 'place of the big pot', a reference to the pool at the foot of the cascade. Fruit and winter vegetables are part of the agricultural bounty of Magoebaskloof and tea is also grown extensively (3 & 4) – the plantations began in 1963 with the help of Kenyan expertise and Industrial Development Corporation money.

1

The splendours of the Transvaal Drakensberg. The Great Escarpment runs north to south for 300 kilometres through the eastern Transvaal, a jagged, majestically spectacular range of mountains and chasms dividing Highveld from Lowveld. The Blyde River Canyon (1) is one of the natural wonders of Africa, falling almost sheer for 800 metres from the great flat-topped buttress of Mariepskop and its trio of companion peaks, the Three Rondavels, to the river below. The Blyde River (4), a tributary of the Olifants, takes its name from the Afrikaans word for 'joy'.

It was here, in 1841, that a party of Voortrekker women, believing themselves to be widows when their reconnoitering menfolk failed to return (the women had already named its sister river 'Treur', which means 'sorrow'), were unexpectedly and joyously reunited. One of the main routes of access to the area is via the Abel Erasmus Pass, where russet-leaved mountain syringas (3) clothe the slopes down to the road. Not surprisingly, the region is a mecca for hikers and holiday-makers, the Blydepoort Dam (2) and resort (5) being especially popular.

Spectacular views abound as one follows the eastern Transvaal Escarpment, among them Pinnacle Rock (1) and two of the loveliest of many waterfalls, Lisbon (5) and Berlin (6). The charming town of Pilgrim's Rest (2 & 3) was a thriving little mining community in the 1870s. As one of the Transvaal's first gold-rush towns, it drew diggers from as far afield as California and Australia, and at one time boasted 21 stores, 18 canteens, three bakeries and a spirited, sometimes outrageous, social life. There were some notable finds here (including a 6 038-gram nugget) and at the quaintly named neighbouring sites of Waterfall Gully, Peach Tree

6

Creek and, farther away, Spitskop and Mac Mac. But gold production began to decline after 1876 and gradually, through the decades, the area was given over to forestry, though a few tiny mines still operate **(4)** and ever-hopeful prospectors continue to pan the streams. The town itself, now reduced to around 630 souls, remains as it once was, virtually untouched by time, a living museum. Also linked to the region's gold rush lore are the Bourke's Luck Potholes **(7)**, strikingly unusual examples of water erosion at the confluence of the Blyde and Treur rivers. It was here that Tom Bourke panned the river and found a fortune in nuggets.

Looking across the mountains from Long Tom Pass towards Sabie (1). The pass, now tarred, its gradients well planned and a popular tourist drive, was once the ruggedly precarious transport route from the eastern Transvaal centre of Lydenburg to the Portuguese East African port of Lourenço Marques (now Maputo, capital of Mozambique). The pass was named after the huge 'Long Tom' 15 cm-calibre Creusot field guns used with devastating effect against the British during the Anglo-Boer War. In September 1900 General Sir Redvers Buller, advancing northwards after relieving Ladysmith, occupied Lydenburg but met with fierce resistance from the remnants of the Boer forces, whose rearguard action in the tortuous Devil's Knuckles area of the high Transvaal Drakensberg kept the Gordon Highlanders at bay for two costly days.

The Sudwala Caves (2 & 3), embedded in a mountain massif known as Mankelekele (which means 'crag on crag'), close to the Crocodile River, are a geological wonder and prime tourist attraction. Rainwater filtering through the dolomite rock over aeons created the lofty chambers of the caves and their festoons of stalagmites and stalactites. One chamber is 90 metres long, 45 metres wide and its formations are of blue, emerald green and pure white. It is said that the labyrinths extend some 30 kilometres.

The stately Elands River Falls **(4)** near Waterval Boven. Here Paul Kruger's Eastern Railway negotiated the Escarpment, linking the Transvaal Republic with the port of Lourenço Marques, now Maputo. Started in 1887 as an attempt to break the British communications stranglehold, it reached the area in 1894 at the cost of countless lives: fever, predatory animals, alcohol and work-gang violence took tragic toll of the workforce. The protected tree fern **(5)** is a common sight in the region.

The eastern Transvaal Lowveld is game country, last sanctuary of the once-teeming hills and plains of the great interior. Biggest of all the country's reserves – larger in extent than Israel – is the world-renowned Kruger National Park, a 19 585 square-kilometre stretch of bushveld sprawling over the north-east part of South Africa that plays host to more than 500 000 visitors a year. Its 15 rest camps, ranging from tiny Roodewal to Skukuza, which is more a self-contained village than a wilderness camp, are designed for comfortable, inexpensive family holidays rather than for the rugged safari. The region is one of the subcontinent's few remaining havens for the big cats.

2

3

4

5

7

6

Around 300 cheetahs **(1 & 2)** live in the Kruger National Park. These cousins to the secretive leopard **(3)** are longer-legged, swifter (they can move at up to 110 km/h) and prefer the relatively few patches of open country to dense bush, as they hunt by outrunning prey and need room in which to move. King of the cats, though, is the lion **(4-7)**. This magnificent male **(6)** was photographed in Timbavati, one of a scatter of smaller, privately owned reserves along Kruger's western border. Most of these adjacent reserves are dense with game; their lodges are in the luxury class and cater to the wealthier game viewer. Timbavati is no exception, but has an added attraction – it is one of the few areas that harbours the rare and beautiful white lion **(4)** – not an albino (its eyes have colour, though its coat is snowy) but rather the product of a recessive gene.

The northern segment of the Kruger National Park is the meeting place of a number of Africa's major ecosystems, and the countryside is one of dramatic contrasts: splendid hills, deep valleys and river gorges; wetland and dry bush; thick forest and open plain; lava flat and soft sand. Water is plentiful; the wildlife prolific. Here in the northern park is the lushly-fringed Luvuvhu River (1) where the visitor is certain to see nyala, hippo (4) and, if lucky, the beautiful but shy bushbuck (5). There are about a thousand bushbuck in the Kruger National Park but they are seldom seen as they tend to browse at night, early in the morning and during the late afternoon, and rest up during the day. There is a great deal of variation in size and coloration within the species: about 40 distinct forms are thought to exist, ranging in colour from dark, unmarked brown to spotted and striped chestnut. Birdlife also abounds and the whitefronted bee-eater (2), with its dragon-fly prey, is but one of 450 species occurring in the park.

4

5

6

A male waterbuck is a lone intruder as a herd of impala mills around at Orpen Dam (3) towards the south of the park. Impala (see also 6) are almost synonymous with the Kruger National Park: the park holds around 160 000 of these graceful antelope and visitors tend to take them for granted. They do, though, merit a closer look from game-viewers, both for their agility and their behaviour patterns. An impala can leap three metres high without apparent effort; a startled herd of several hundred will cover the ground as one in a swift, flowing, instinctively choreographed movement that surprises and delights the eye. The group organization is complex: normally gentle and gregarious animals, adult males become fiercely competitive and territorial in the mating season.

The warthog (**1**) is not the handsomest of Nature's children, but what it lacks in looks it makes up for in toughness and instinct for self-preservation: the tusks are razor-sharp, the senses of smell and hearing acute. Grazers for the most part, these animals can also live on wild fruits, tubers and roots.

A tree leguaan (**2**) is not pretty either. Leguaans, of which there are two species in southern Africa (the other is the Nile monitor) are prized by local herbalists for the curative properties of their skin and fat. The tree species has a curious defence mechanism: when molested it will feign death rather than attempt escape.

A kudu bull (**3**) browses in the Kruger National Park. The kudu is among the largest of Africa's antelopes, lives in family groups of about a dozen and, in the mating season, is fiercely territorial: fights between competing bulls can be fatal. The long, spiral horns take about six years to reach their full size.

White rhino (**4**) occur in the Kruger National Park as well as in the adjacent Londolozi game reserve (part of the extensive Sabie-Sand reserve) where these specimens were photographed. The white rhino is, after the elephant, the second largest of the land mammals, the males weighing up to 3,5 tons. Aggressive enough in looks, the white rhino is not nearly as belligerent as its rarer cousin, the black rhino, though it will mock charge if alarmed.

Wild Dogs (**5**) are a common sight in the Kruger National Park. These gregarious animals hunt in packs, relentlessly pursuing their quarry until they run it down.

One of the park's major rivers is the Olifants (**6**). The Olifants rest camp, set on rocky cliffs a full hundred metres above the river, is particularly attractive. Visitors enjoy stunning views of the hills and valleys and (with binoculars) the prolific wildlife drawn to the lush riverine vegetation.

5

6

Camp life. An aerial view of Letaba (1), in the central region of the Kruger National Park, at the strategic junction of the three major roads and well placed above a sweeping bend in the Great Letaba River. Elephant, buffalo, zebra, hippo, crocodile and many species of antelope can all be viewed from the comfort of the camp's pleasant terraces. Letaba's rondavels (2) are unpretentious, comfortable and equipped with the essentials for cooking and eating, though there is a central restaurant.

Skukuza is the largest camp in the Kruger National Park and here elaborate displays (**3**) educate visitors in the ways of the wild.

In the Sabie-Sand Private Nature Reserve, dinner in the *boma* (**4**) is a highlight of a stay at the Mala Mala Lodge, as is game viewing from an open Land Rover (**5**). But the private reserves also offer visitors the opportunity to 'rough it', and at Timbavati guests enjoy a bush breakfast (**6**) near Tanda Tula Lodge while hikers set out from the M'Bali tented camp (**7**) in Umbabat.

1

Giraffes **(1)** are among the more common sights in the southern parts of the Kruger National Park, the largest concentration being near the Satara and Crocodile Bridge camps. They have just one natural enemy: the lion. Despite their size (as much as six metres tall and weighing up to 1,5 tons), giraffes are masters of camouflage, blending well with their dappled surroundings.

The Kruger National Park's smaller fry include the tree squirrel **(2)** and lesser-masked weavers **(3)**, arguably the most adept of all nest-builders. Among the park's many species of antelope are the waterbuck **(4)**, with their shaggy grey coats and the telltale white circle around the rump, and the roan **(5)**, one of the rarest species in the park. Crocodiles **(6)** are common in the park's rivers and are a constant threat to animals quenching their thirst.

The chacma baboon **(1)** is everywhere in the Kruger National Park; in fact it is common throughout the country. It is inquisitive, cunning, and not above stealing from visitors' cars.

The park has a population of some 25 000 buffalo **(2 & 5)** – a healthy figure, as eight decades ago the species almost became extinct when rinderpest devastated the herds. Outwardly placid, the buffalo is nevertheless one of the most dangerous of animals when wounded or molested. The big predators tend to leave them alone, but when a herd does come under threat it forms a defensive ring, very much like a laager.

The blue wildebeest **(3)** is also fairly abundant in the park, as is the whitebacked vulture **(4)**, a voracious scavenger which is quick to arrive at the scene of death. This summer-nesting species lays a single egg, incubated by both parents.

3   4

1

2

3

Elephants are among the most endearing of all animals and are often responsible for halting traffic in the Kruger National Park as visitors jockey for photographs (1). Although old males tend to live alone, elephants are social animals and live in family units – a mother and her offspring – which may group together to form herds (2 & 3).

Because elephants have huge appetites and are generally destructive feeders – they will often push over fully grown trees to reach a few succulent shoots – they devastate the land, threatening not only

5

the survival of other animals but themselves as well, unless their numbers are controlled. To this end annual censuses are taken and, where necessary, the animals are culled. This long-term management programme has stabilized the elephant population of the Kruger National Park at around 7 500, the majority living in the mopane-covered northern region. The mopane is a favourite food source and here (5) an adult strips a young shrub.

These gregarious giants of the veld are often near water as, like everything else about them, their daily intake is huge – about 130 litres for an adult. Family groups are commonly seen at the Kruger National Park's rivers, including the Letaba (4).

The park's elephants are notable for their unusually large tusks: over 20 bulls have been counted with one or both weighing more than 50 kg. One magnificent specimen, the late and lamented Mafunyane ('the irritable one'), had tusks as heavy as this, a prime prize for poachers.

4

5

The Free State's plains tend to be bare, sparsely populated, undulating prairie land, epitomized by the lonely road between Ficksburg and Fouriesburg (1). It is the breadbasket of the country, with some 30 000 farms given over to wheat and maize as well as sheep and cattle. Livestock auctions, such as this one at Heilbron (2), are important events in the farming calendar. Water is scarce, and underground sources lifted from below by windmills (3) are often the principal supply rather than the supplementary.

Bethlehem (4), with the sandstone foothills of the Maluti Mountains in the distance, is typical of the Orange Free State's country towns: neat collections of unpretentious bungalows huddled around main street and Dutch Reformed church, surrounded by the dun vastness of a treeless land. When it does rain, the veld greens quickly, as it has done around this Sotho kraal in the Rooiberg range (5).

Bloemfontein, the Orange Free State's only city and the Republic's judicial capital, was founded in 1846, when the Great Trek was eight years old and thousands of Cape settlers had crossed the Orange River in search of a new country. The seat of government was the Old Raadsaal (3), a modest building but palatial compared to the *hartbeeshuis* (2) in the grounds of the Old Presidency. This rude dwelling is a reconstruction of the home of the Brits family, on whose farm the capital was built.

A good view (5) of the central city with its contemporary and mostly uninspired architecture is gained from the top of nearby Naval Hill. There are, however, several imposing buildings of more elegant proportions such as the Afrikaans Literature Museum (1).

Despite its agricultural emphasis, the Free State has its share of heavy industry. The Sasolburg oil-from-coal plant (4), for example, was built by the South African Oil and Gas Corporation, in the 1960s, on a huge coalfield just south of the Vaal River. Of slightly earlier vintage are the vast goldfields around the town of Welkom, which was established in 1947 and now has a population of 150 000. Such operations are not necessarily detrimental to Nature in every respect: this pan (the water is pumped from the mines) provides a fine feeding ground for a flock of flamingoes (6).

The Golden Gate Highlands National Park, one of South Africa's 14 national parks, is an almost 5 000-hectare tract of rugged sandstone uplands in the Orange Free State, 360 kilometres south of Johannesburg. Famed for the shapes and colours (much is indeed golden) of its stark, hauntingly beautiful sandstone formations such as the Brandwag Rock **(1)** and the Mushroom

Rocks **(3)**, the park also offers a splendid variety of bright wild flowers (fire and arum lilies, red hot pokers, watsonias), and of birdlife (the raptors, including the rare lammergeyer, are especially noteworthy), and is a paradise for climbers, riders and walkers, the two-day Rhebuck Trail **(2)** being particularly popular.

4

5

The park is also home to the black wildebeest **(4)**, easily identified by its white tail. In fact the species is also known as the white-tailed gnu – gnu being a corruption of a Hottentot word which imitates the whistling sound the animal makes when alarmed.

Brandwag Lodge **(5)** offers sophistication in a rural setting: a fine restaurant and cocktail bar, luxury double and single rooms, as well as fully equipped family chalets.

South Africa's largest river, and principal source of water in a generally dry land, is the Orange, which rises high in the Drakensberg and rolls its way westward for 2 000 kilometres to the Atlantic Ocean, bringing sustenance to the otherwise arid northern regions of the Karoo, Bushmanland and the north-western Cape. Principal reservoir of the river's water is the 374 square-kilometre Hendrik Verwoerd Dam, which irrigates extensive areas of the Free State and, by means of two tunnels running southwards (one of 89 km, the other of 52 km), supplies much-needed replenishment to the Fish and Sundays rivers. The dam's resort **(6)** is a popular holiday venue.

6

Mountains of the dragon. The Great Escarpment reaches its most dramatic heights in the east, where the towering faces of the Natal Drakensberg rise, sometimes almost sheer, 3 000 and more metres from the plains of the Natal midlands. One access is via the foothills in the Witsieshoek region (2) bordering the Orange Free State and the tiny national state of Qwa Qwa. The Tugela River rises near Mont-aux-

Sources – at 3 282 metres, the highest of the Natal peaks – and after finding its way through the upper slopes (3) plunges 600 metres down the escarpment, through the magnificent Royal Natal National Park, with the ramparts of the Amphitheatre as its backdrop (1), and then meanders through 250 kilometres of often desiccated countryside to the eastern seaboard.

The Amphitheatre's Eastern Buttress, with its attendant Devil's Tooth **(4)**, is just one of the countless climbing challenges that draw mountaineers from all over the country, indeed the world. The Natal Parks are renowned for their comfortable but unobtrusive accommodation, and Tendele Camp **(5)** is no exception.

1

South of the Royal Natal National Park are two heights of special splendour: Mnweni, or 'place of fingers', but commonly known as the Rockeries (3 116 metres) and, farther on, an eastward-projecting ridge of lofty peaks: Cathedral; Bell; Outer Horn; Inner Horn, and smaller ones known as the Mitre and the Chessmen. Views everywhere are spectacular, none more so than through the Map of Africa (1) and up the winter-browned slopes of the 'Little Berg' towards Cathedral peak (4).

But in the 'Berg, beauty lies not only in the grand panorama: everywhere wild flowers delight the eye: *Helichrysum* spp. (2 & 3); *Hesperantha* spp. (5 & 7) and the delicate cream and yellow *Protea subvestita* (6).

At the foot of the Natal Drakensberg lies the 35 000-hectare Giant's Castle Game Reserve, a natural paradise of grassy slopes and deep river valleys presided over by the basalt massifs of Champagne Castle, the Trojan Wall, eNjesuthi and, most majestic of all, the 3 314-metre high Giant's Castle itself, standing in stark whiteness above the Bushman's River (5). The reserve is home to a number of antelope species, including the stately eland (1) as well as smaller denizens such as the common girdled lizard (2) and common night adder (3). The Giant's Castle rest camp, in a setting of wild flowers, is especially attractive, and there are mountain huts for hikers, climbers, riders, trout fishermen and bird watchers. Lone Basotho horsemen (4) are not an uncommon sight in the high mountain passes.

The deep pink flowerhead of *Watsonia meriana* (**1**), a welcome splash of colour high in the 'Berg where the Sani Pass (**2**) makes its tortuous way up the escarpment. The pass, one of a few linking Natal with the land-locked mountain kingdom of Lesotho, is the highest in south-ern Africa, some 2 900 m above sea level at its summit.

Bushmen once hunted and gathered food in the foothills of the Drakensberg and made their

homes in the many shallow caves and rock shelters at the base of sandstone cliffs. They are long gone, but their art, one of the land's greatest treasures, remains. The smooth surface of the rock gave them an ideal 'canvas' for its expression and the hunting scene depicted here (**3**) is part of one of the many galleries to be seen throughout the Natal Drakensberg. In the Main Caves, at Giant's Castle, is a reconstruction of how Bushmen lived in their shelters (**4**).

The towering crags are a constant challenge to rock climbers but, for the less adventurous, the grassy lower slopes are criss-crossed with tracks to be explored (**5**).

The Zulu people number between six and seven million, and are the largest of southern Africa's ethnic groupings. Their 'homeland' is KwaZulu, a patchwork of territories scattered about Natal, self-governing but not yet fully independent: Chief Minister Mangosuthu Buthelezi and his government would prefer an integrated South African state in which power is shared rather than divided. Much of the land is over-grazed and poor, with erosion an ever-present threat. The 'beehive' huts (3) are quintessentially Zulu. Facilities for the large rural population are for the most part woefully inadequate – the river is often the only source for household water (1) and transport frequently an ox-drawn sledge (4).

The Zulus, most powerful and warlike of the 19th century black nations, have a proud history and strong cultural traditions, though many of the latter are being eroded by western industrial influences. The 'warrior' (2) is costumed for the tourist's benefit; but the young woman (5) is dressed in the distinctive manner sometimes still seen in the Ixopo region of southern Natal.

1

2

3

4

5

The daily round in KwaZulu. A woman makes a hide skirt **(3)** while others prepare reed bundles for thatching **(1)**; children attend an open-air primary school **(4)** and a matron in more traditional dress visits the local store **(5)**. Huts dot the rolling hills close to the Transkei border **(2)**.

4

5

Natal's English heritage is evident everywhere but especially in the country areas where 'the club' and polo (2) are well supported; the colonial traditions are loyally, sometimes aggressively preserved.

Reminders of a troubled past are these relics of Anglo-Zulu conflict during the 1870s (3).

Although cattle are farmed extensively in the Natal midlands (4), sugar (1) has been one of Natal's economic mainstays since the first of thousands of indentured Indian labourers arrived in the 1860s.

The Howick Falls (5), on the Mgeni River before it winds through the Valley of a Thousand Hills, are among the country's loveliest.

1

2

6

Pietermaritzburg **(1)**, the capital of Natal, is a charming city, albeit a small one, nestled in the misty uplands some 90 kilometres inland from the coast. Colonial influences are strong here, too, and like Durban, 'Maritzburg has a substantial Indian community **(2)**. Among the city's places of interest are the Botanic Gardens **(4)** which have a 46-metre high fig tree, a splendid avenue of planes and a great wealth of indigenous and exotic plantlife.

A modern dual-carriage highway now links Pietermaritzburg with Durban, but for those not in too much of a hurry to reach the beach, the old road, a narrow ribbon that wends its way up hill and down dale, provides an alternative route. The scenery is splendid, especially the Valley of a Thousand Hills **(5)**. Most prominent of its features is Natal's Table Mountain, a flat-topped 658-metre high massif whose summit (easily reached from the western side) offers unrivalled views. The 'old road' is also the route of the annual Comrades Marathon, one of the most punishing of the world's ultra long-distance runs **(6)**. Also worthy of attention and not too far off the motorway is the Mariannhill Monastery **(3)**.

South Africa's playground. Durban is the country's largest port, third largest city, busy centre of industry and commerce, and paradise for pleasure-seekers – especially from the land-locked Transvaal, some seven hours' drive away. Its beachfront **(1-5)** is a three-kilometre strip of modern hotels, an aquarium, bowling greens, playgrounds, amusement parks, gardens, paddling pools, tearooms, some excellent restaurants, a mini-town (scale 1:24), fishing jetties, and magnificent golden beaches sloping steeply into the warm, roller-waved Indian Ocean.

4

5

4

5

6

7

Tourism is Durban's most obvious industry and during the holiday seasons the city is invaded by up-country folk eager for the sea, a tan, and fun. The beachfront amusement centre (1 & 3) and the slides at Waterworld (2) provide plenty of the latter. While the city caters well to the masses there is an impressive range of luxury accommodation (4) for the more affluent. The rickshaws (5), each drawn by a Zulu in imposing regalia (the costume is an imaginative invention, not traditional garb) are as much part of the beachfront scene as candyfloss and icecream (6) and Zulu handicrafts (7).

Durban's harbour (1-4). The bay is almost land-locked; the entrance narrow and, until the turn of the century, blocked to ocean-going ships by an unpredictably shifting sandbar. The harbour now handles over half the cargo passing through South Africa's ports. It is also home to the Royal Natal Yacht Club (3).

The City Hall (5) dominates the central business district and, lending authority to its late-Victorian style is a statue to the old Queen (8) in an adjacent park. She would not have been amused by the punk fashions of these girls waiting for a bus (6). The City Hall has an excellent library, art gallery, museum (housing, among other intriguing exhibits, the most complete skeleton in existence of the extinct dodo) and an auditorium seating 2 500 people. Adding a splash of colour to the city centre are the flower sellers (7) in front of the Post Office.

Eastern, Western and African cultures co-exist in Durban, giving the city a mix that is unique, vibrant and sometimes volatile. Glimpses of this milieu are: the Grey Street Mosque (**1**), the largest in the southern hemisphere (the tall white building in the background is the new beachfront Holiday Inn); a scene at the municipal market (**2**); a spice hall at the Oriental Bazaar (**3**); a Hindu wedding (**4**); golf at the Country Club (**5**); chess in Medwood Gardens (**6**); a Sunday afternoon boxing match (**7**); and an enthusiastic soccer crowd (**8**) at the stadium at Umlazi, one of Durban's satellite black townships.

5

6

7

8

4

Leaving Durban on the North Coast road the traveller passes a string of towns and attractive resorts, but within a few hours the scene changes dramatically as one enters the realm of Zululand's reserves – each remarkable for its beauty and wildlife. None is more so than St Lucia, a vast system of lakes, coastal forests and dunes. Not surprisingly, wildlife is prolific and the visitor is assured of good sightings of hippo, crocodiles, flamingoes and pelicans (1). Among the many camps is picturesque Charter's Creek (2), a complex of self-contained rondavels and cottages. Angling (3), too, is excellent and fishermen are drawn to the area from all over the country, but it is Sodwana Bay (5) to the north of St Lucia that is arguably the mecca for South Africa's angling fraternity. Among the many smaller creatures found along the Zululand coast are fiddler crabs such as this specimen (4).

5

1

2

Inland from the coast is the renowned Umfolozi Game Reserve which takes its name from the Black (**4**) and the White Umfolozi rivers. The name Umfolozi means 'zig-zag', an apt name for these two rivers which wander widely and then meet in this unspoilt land. Umfolozi is home not only to the world's largest concentration of white rhino but also to the black rhino (**6**).

3

4

Lions (**1**) also roam the reserve as does the stately nyala (**3**) which in Zululand reaches the southern limit of its distribution. Birdlife is prolific, and includes the hadeda ibis (**2**) which fills the morning and evening air with its raucous call. Insects form the bulk of the hadeda's diet, but a pyrgomorphid locust (**5**) is safe enough because of its foul taste.

5

6

Farther north, through a gap in the Lebombo mountains, lies the Mkuzi Game Reserve, as rich in the variety of its vegetation as in its animal life. Giant sycamore figs (**2**) are a feature of the park, as are its many watercourses and shallow sweetwater pans which sustain the reserve's inhabitants: cheetah (**1**), grey heron (**3**), African jacana (**4**), and the white rhino (**5**) to name but a few.

3

4

5

The white rhino once occurred widely in Africa, but with the expansion of 19th century settlement, the indiscriminate predations of sporting hunters and of superstitious poachers (quite erroneously, the rhino's horn is thought to have aphrodisiac properties) the numbers declined to the point where the species faced extinction. By the turn of the century there were just 30 specimens left, tucked into the 250 square-kilometre patch of Zululand territory between the two arms of the Umfolozi River. The tide of destruction was turned, however, with the creation of the Umfolozi Game Reserve. Official sanctuary saved the animals, and the numbers grew to such an extent that they began to pose a threat to their habitat. But with the development of immobilizing drugs and capture techniques, the Natal Parks Board started to 'export' the animals to depleted areas such as Mkuzi, the Kruger National Park and farther afield. By the 1980s well over 3 000 white rhino had found new homes.

Mkuzi's Msinga waterhole is one of two in the reserve where visitors can view game from a comfortable hide (**3**). The cool of early morning and late evening are the best viewing times and patience is rewarded as the animals come down to slake their thirst, among them kudu (**1**), warthogs (**2**) and zebra (**4**). Birds, too, are found in abundance at the waterholes, but for wetland birds few places can compete with the huge Nsumu Pan (**5**) at the confluence of the Mkuze and Umsunduzi rivers.

1

2

3

4

5

6

Ndumu (**1-6**) is the northernmost of the Zululand reserves, lying along South Africa's border with Mozambique nearly 500 kilometres from Durban. It is not a big reserve but what it lacks in size it makes up for in quality – Ndumu's 11 000-hectare floodplain is an intricate lattice of freshwater pans, such as Nyamithi (**6**) where no fewer than 393 bird species have been recorded, many of them tropical species which reach the southern limit of their ranges here. The goliath heron (**5**) is not one of the rarer species of Ndumu – it is fairly common in many wetland areas – but few can fail to be impressed by its sheer size; mature birds can grow to 1,4 metres and have a wingspan of about 1,2 metres. Not surprisingly, the reserve attracts 'birders' from far beyond the country's borders, but botanists, too, are well rewarded, for among the many plant species is *Encephalartos ferox* (**1**), a member of the ancient cycad family, living fossils which have inhabited the earth for over 200 million years. Comparative newcomers to the stage, but no less impressive, are the sycamore figs (**4**).

In sharp contrast to the pristine reserves of Zululand is the almost continuous string of resort towns along the coast south of Durban towards the Transkei border. Among them are Margate (**3 & 5**) and Ramsgate (**4**) where the holiday-maker has everything to hand: safe bathing from beaches protected by shark nets, good surf, good fishing (**1**), and countless places to eat. For those needing respite, however, a day drive to the Oribi Gorge area is a delightful interlude. Here the Umzimkulu River carves its way through rolling hills, providing some spectacular scenery such as the view from the towering 'Walls of Jericho' (**2**).

Just over the Transkei border is the Wild Coast Casino, a Sun City-type complex with a world-renowned golf course (**6**), Waterworld (**7**) and luxury hotel (**8**). Transkei, a national state, is poorly endowed with natural resources and relies heavily on tourism to balance its budget.

6

7

8

The Transkei is a poor country, its people mainly rural and eking a living from over-used land. From the main route through the Transkei, inland and via the capital of Umtata, branch a number of rough gravel roads leading to remote coastal villages, *en route* winding through rolling hills dotted with limewashed Xhosa homes (**1**), a region where people in traditional garb – older women often smoking their characteristically long pipes (**2**) – are a common sight. The undulating landscape ends abruptly at one of southern Africa's greatest scenic treasures, the Wild Coast, a challenge for

hikers (**5**) and a place for those who like their holidays to be simple and private. It is a lonely, strikingly beautiful shoreline of unspoilt beaches, estuaries and towering cliffs weathered into fantastic shapes such as Cathedral Rock (**3**), the Fallen Idol (**4**) and Waterfall Bluff (**6**) where one can walk between the rock face and the cascade plunging directly into the sea.

Quiet and restful, East London straddles the estuary of the Buffalo River in a narrow corridor of land sandwiched between the republics of Transkei to the east and Ciskei to the west. It is South Africa's only river port (1 & 2), handling outgoing citrus, mineral ores and wool as well as imports destined mainly for the Orange Free State. East London's immediate coastline comprises a string of sandy beaches – the Orient is said to be one of the safest in the country for bathers, while the Eastern (7) is more popular with surfers and anglers (4) – linked by rocky points with their intriguing inter-tidal pools (3). Even the business centre is relaxed, presided over by a stately city

1

2

3

4

5

6

7

hall, a monument to colonial forces who fell during the Anglo-Boer War **(6)** at its entrance.

Some 70 kilometres inland from East London is King William's Town, which had its beginning in 1835 as a garrison outpost built on the site of a mission station. Dressed stone is very much a feature of King William's Town's architecture – as indeed it is throughout the eastern Cape – and there are many fine, sturdy old buildings, including the Holy Trinity Church **(5)**, built in 1856.

Grahamstown, its skyline dominated by the spire of the Cathedral of St Michael and St George **(1)**, is the heart of English-speaking South Africa. For it was to this region, the scene of many bloody frontier wars, that some 4 000 British immigrants

were brought to settle and thereby provide a 'buffer' between the Cape Colony and the Xhosa-speaking tribes to the east. The statue (2) is part of the 1820 Settlers' National Monument which stands atop Gunfire Hill overlooking the city. Grahamstown started life in the early 19th century as a garrison, and faced its first great challenge in April 1819 when close on 10 000 Xhosa warriors descended on the outpost. It survived this and other crises, and over the years assumed its more peaceful Victorian character, a character which persists to this day (3). For obvious reasons Grahamstown is known as the Settler City, but it is also called the City of Saints – there are over 40 churches – and the City of Schools for its many places of learning, including Rhodes University (4).

The scattering of small towns and villages around Grahamstown are also redolent with their English heritage, none more so than Bathurst, complete with its 'Pig 'n Whistle' pub (5). The road from the village leads to Port Alfred on the Kowie River (7), a quiet, pleasant coastal resort, renowned for its lovely shoreline, especially popular with shell collectors: more than 1 800 shell species have been found in the area.

Typical of the eastern Cape landscape is this scene (6): gently rolling hills with lonely roads 'switchbacking' along their contours.

5

6

7

Port Elizabeth's history dates back to 1799, when the new British regime built Fort Frederick on the slopes overlooking Algoa Bay, then at the extremity of the Cape Colony's frontier. It was here, on the shores of the Bay, that the 1820 Settlers made their lonely landfall. Today the city, economic hub of the Eastern Cape, is one of the major industrial centres of South Africa and boasts the country's third largest harbours (3-4). Despite the focus on industry, however, Port Elizabeth is a friendly place with much to offer the visitor: fine buildings – the

1

2

3

4

5

6

7

elegant Public Library (2) and the terrace of Victorian Settler homes (5) being but two examples – and a snake park (1) which houses over 1 000 reptiles (public demonstrations have halted after the death of a handler some years ago). Next door is a museum and an oceanarium.

A highlight of any visit to Port Elizabeth is a day trip to the Addo Elephant National Park (6), haven for the last of the once-great Cape herds. It was here, in the early years of the century, that the unequal contest between farmer and wild animal was finally resolved. The survivors – some 10 elephants – fled to the impenetrable 'hunter's hell' region between the Zuurberg and the Sundays River valley; today, the park's elephant population is three times denser than anywhere else in Africa.

South-westwards from Port Elizabeth, St Francis Bay sweeps in a gentle arc – 100 km of smooth, sandy beaches (7), resorts, holiday cottages, and a sea tailor-made for surfers and fishermen. Also to the west of Port Elizabeth the national road passes through verdant farmlands near Humansdorp (8), gateway to the Garden Route.

8

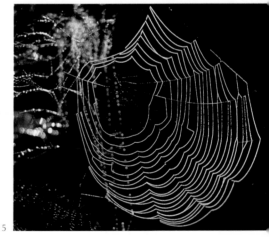

The Cape's Garden Route, 230 kilometres from Storms River to Mossel Bay in the west, is one of the loveliest coastal strips in the world. Here there are beaches and bays, imposing cliffs, mountains, and everywhere the deep green of forest. What French explorer le Vaillant wrote of the area in the 1780s is apt today: 'The land bears the name Outeniqua, which in the Hottentot tongue means "a man laden with honey". The flowers grow there in their millions, the mixture of pleasant scents which arises from them, their colour, their variety, the pure and fresh air which one breathes there, all make one stop and think nature has made an enchanted abode of this beautiful place.'

Capturing some of the magic of the area are: *Erica chloroloma* (**1**); a giant yellowwood tree (**2**) in the Grootrivier Pass; the Knysna loerie (**3**), seldom seen but its loud, booming cry fills the forest; the vivid bracket fungus *Pycnoporus cinnabarinus* (**4**); a dew-laden spider's web (**5**); the ubiquitous rock hyrax (**6**); Nature's Valley lagoon (**7**); setting up camp in the Tsitsikamma Coastal National Park (**8**); and a baboon perched at the crown of a tall *Strelitzia* tree (**9**).

Within little more than a decade Plettenberg Bay has grown from a sleepy village to a bustling town packed to capacity during the summer season with holiday-makers from the coastal cities as well as upcountry. Eating places abound (**2**) and there is Beacon Isle, a hotel and time-sharing complex (**1**) perched on a rocky promontory in the bay. But for those who enjoy simpler pursuits, 'Plett', with its magnificent sweep of sandy beach and the lagoon of the Bietou River (**3**), offers superb angling, safe bathing and surfing – the bay is sheltered from the south by the Robberg, a high red-sandstone peninsula.

Thirty kilometres along the coast west of Plettenberg Bay is the pretty town of Knysna, lying on the shores of a vast lagoon and inland surrounded by dense brooding forests and fertile farmland (7). In an area famous for its natural beauty the sandstone heads (1), which guard the narrow access to the lagoon, are a highlight, while the lagoon (3 & 4) is itself a paradise for fishermen, divers, boating enthusiasts and windsurfers. Marine scientists also take a great interest in the lagoon, for it is an important nursery for a number of fish species and is also home to a rare sea horse.

The history of Knysna cannot be told without reference to George Rex who played a central role in the development of the town. Rex, an eccentric early 19th century English settler, lived in the area in grandly

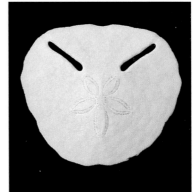

aristocratic, almost regal style, leaving behind a large family and a wealth of legend. His grave (2) lies on his farm Melkhoutkraal.

Between Knysna and the Wilderness lies another, even more extensive system of lakes and lagoons which provide sanctuary for birdlife such as the greater flamingo (5) as well as holiday playgrounds such as Pine Lake Marina (6) on the shores of Swartvlei.

The delicate pansy shell (8) is in fact not a shell but the exoskeleton of a sand-dwelling animal. Although synonymous with the Garden Route coast, it is found in estuarine conditions from Cape Infanta at the mouth of the Breede River to Durban.

The Garden Route continues: Swart-vlei's outlet to the sea near Sedgefield (1); a stream stained dark by rotting vegetation meanders through indigenous forest (2); sheltered Herold's Bay with its cluster of holiday homes (3); and great loops of golden beaches (4 & 5).

West of Sedgefield and the Wilderness is the town of George, the imposing Dutch Reformed Church (6) serving its largely Afrikaans-speaking community. (Ironically the town was the first to be established by the British in South Africa.) The town is also the centre of a thriving furniture industry (7) which makes good use of local hardwoods.

The road north from George to Oudtshoorn climbs in spectacular fashion over the Outeniqua Mountains, which rise 1 580 metres to George Peak. This is the dividing line between the narrow coastal zone and the Little Karoo, a barrier that proved nightmarish for the road engineers of the past. There are four major passes, including the Montagu (1), opened in 1847 and still in use. At its foot stands the old toll house (three-halfpence a wheel if you used a patent brake; 3d. a wheel if brakeless) and, half way up, there are the remains of the old and once much-needed blacksmith's repair shop.

The Little Karoo, a basin in the Cape Folded Mountain belt, is a strange world of imposing sandstone mountains, deep ravines, and a profusion of wild flowers including *Aloe ferox* with its fiery orange-red spikes (2). The soil, apparently arid in many places, is in fact very fertile, watered by the perennial streams of the Swartberg to the north and the Langeberg and Outeniqua ranges to the south, and by the Olifants River, which brings rich alluvial soil on its meandering way from the Great Karoo.

Oudtshoorn, principal town of the Little Karoo, was the world's ostrich feather capital, a thriving centre in the days prior to the First World War when plumes – those of the male bird (3) were most highly prized – adorned fashionable headgear. At one time the green lucerne fields of the area supported over 100 000 of the big birds; ostrich farmers made fortunes and built ornate 'feather palaces' (4). Although the ostrich boom is long past, there are still prosperous farms such as this one (5) at the foot of the snow-dusted Swartberg mountains. Feathers continue to be sold by public auction in the town.

4

5

One of southern Africa's most famous natural wonders is the complex of tortuous subterranean passages and chambers known as the Cango Caves. Hundreds of thousands of visitors make the journey each year to the Caves deep in the foothills of the Swartberg, and few fail to be awed by their fantastic dripstone formations (**1 & 2**). The Caves were 'discovered' in the late 1700s, but in

earlier times Bushmen made the entrances to these labyrinths their home, decorating the walls with their marvellous art. Largest of the chambers is the 107-metre-wide Grand Hall.

West of the Little Karoo is the Gamka River valley (**6**), between the Swartberg and Langeberg ranges, popularly known as 'The Hell'. The land is in fact fertile enough, though today only three families farm in this remote area, still laying out their figs (**5**) and other fruit to dry in the hot sun. The old water-driven flour mill (**7**), although no longer in use, is a reminder of a more active past.

Showing glimpses of the agricultural variety in the Little Karoo are this vineyard near Ladismith (**3**) and a farm in the Calitzdorp district (**4**).

4

5

6

7

The thirstlands. In geological terms the Great Karoo, a vast basin stretching from the highveld escarpment in the north to the Little Karoo in the south, is part of the Karoo System, an even more extensive area of deep sedimentary deposits that covers almost two thirds of the subcontinent. It is a country of far horizons interrupted by starkly sculptured dolorite rock formations such as the mountains near Sutherland (1); of blistering days, explosive sunsets and the clearest of nights, and, in springtime, of carpets of bright and hardy mesembryanthemums (2); and of dusty gravel roads plied by donkey-drawn carts (5). There are no perennial streams; flash-storms do more harm than good as the earth is tenuously protected by vegetation and vulnerable to erosion. Much of Laingsburg (6), one of the region's few towns and on the main north-south highway, was destroyed by sudden floods in 1981. But underground water sources are tapped by the ubiquitous wind-pump, sustaining the sheep farms. Sheep farming (3) is synonymous with the Karoo, home to most of southern Africa's 35 million sheep which browse the plains where huge herds of antelope, springbok, eland and hartebeest once roamed unhindered by fences and unmolested by the hunter's gun. There are wildlife sanctuaries, however, largest of which is the Karoo National Park (4) near Beaufort West.

5

6

1

The haunting Valley of Desolation (**1**), 14 kilometres west of Graaff-Reinet in the southern Karoo. The town (**2**) was capital of a rebellious, short-lived 'republic' in the 1790s, and much of its picturesque past has been preserved. Charming Victorian cottages (**3**) line the streets and many buildings have been meticulously restored – more than 200 are national monuments – including an entire street, Stretch's Court (**4**), now part of the Drostdy Hotel.

To the east of Graaff-Reinet, on the northern slopes of the Bankberg near Cradock, is the 6 536-hectare Mountain Zebra National Park (**7**), sanctuary to one of the world's rarest large mammals (**5**). There are also some fine examples of Bushman rock art in the area (**6**).

The 'Great North Road' near Three Sisters **(2)** where the national highway forks right to Bloemfontein and left to Kimberley via the towns of Strydenburg and Hopetown. Strydenburg **(3)** is a typical, tidy little centre of Karoo farming industry whose Afrikaans name translates into 'town of strife', commemorating an acrimonious local quarrel – over what to call the place! The area is one of the last outposts of the steam engine and enthusiasts are likely to be rewarded with the sight of one trailing its cloud of smoke across the veld **(4)**.

2

It was close to Hopetown (1), south of Kimberley in the northern Karoo, that the first significant diamond find was made. In 1866 young Erasmus Jacobs, walking along the banks of the Orange, picked up a 21,25-carat stone (later named the 'Eureka'); three years later a second diamond, the 83-carat 'Star of South Africa' was found and eventually bought by the Earl of Dudley for £30 000. But the diggers who thronged the area found little else of value: the real wealth lay in the kimberlite pipes to the north. Hopetown today is the attractive headquarters of an agricultural region (cattle, sheep, fruit) enriched by the waters of the Orange.

In the far west of the Karoo, bordering the even drier Namaqualand region, is the Akkerendam Nature Reserve (5) in the Hantam mountains near Calvinia. Gemsbok, black wildebeest and the rare Hartmann's mountain zebra live·here and each year the bleak landscape is transformed by the glory of carpets of wild spring flowers.

Diamonds, fabulous deposits of them, were discovered in 1870 in the 'yellow ground' of Colesburg Koppie in the wasteland north of the Orange River, provoking one of the 19th century's most frantic rushes. The koppie was literally torn apart, the 'blue ground' beneath found to contain even richer treasures, and the Big Hole (5) sunk ever deeper, with at times up to 30 000 men working its kimberlite claims. Around the now abandoned Hole grew the town of Kimberley, at first a chaotic collection of tents and shacks, canteens, doss-houses and dusty streets swarming with unkempt humanity; later, after the claims had been consolidated, it became an orderly and attractive town that has preserved much of its romantic past.

Diamonds are still mined in the area (1), and these, together with all other diamonds mined in South Africa and Namibia, are sorted at Kimberley's tall Harry Oppenheimer House, here forming the backdrop to the Digger Fountain (3) in the Oppenheimer Memorial Gardens.

A highlight of a visit to Kimberley is the 'living' museum where buildings and their interiors (2) have been reconstructed to capture something of the flavour of Old Kimberley. Reminders of the town's heyday are such homes as Melrose House (4) and the Kimberley Club (6), still very much in use and where Cecil Rhodes dreamed of empires.

Far to the south-west of Kimberley is Prieska on the banks of the Orange River; the grim stone fort with kokerboom sentries (7) is a relic of the Anglo-Boer War.

1

Centrepiece of the Augrabies National Park, a 9 000-hectare wilderness area around the lower reaches of the Orange River near the Namibian border, is the Augrabies gorge (1), a nine-kilometre long, deep granite cleft through which the river, during one short stretch, plunges 146 metres to a deep pool in a series of spectacular cataracts. The main fall and the subsidiary Bridal Veil fall (3) are some 93 metres high. At peak periods the volume of water over the main Augrabies cataract is more than

half that of the mighty Victoria Falls in flood, but is dramatically concentrated across a far narrower width. Best viewing is from the north bank of the river.

The Klipspringer Trail, a long but undemanding hike through the southern area of the park, is a great attraction. It takes its name from the medium-sized antelope (2) whose sure-footedness makes it ideally adapted to the rocky terrain. In the dry scrubland of the region, the tall kokerboom (4) stands out, often adorned with the straggly 'condominium' nests of sociable weavers.

Some 250 kilometres north of Augrabies, in the great, infinitely remote tract of red duneland (2) is the Kalahari Gemsbok National Park which has a boundary, unrestricted by fences, with an even larger reserve in Botswana. Nearly a million hectares in extent, much of the national park is a virtually inaccessible wasteland of aeolian sand supporting hardy shrubs and scatterings of acacia (3).

But the aridity is deceptive, especially towards the western parts where the Auob River flows (albeit very seldom) and there is hidden water sustaining a varied wildlife. For example, in the Kalahari Gemsbok National Park more than 200 species of bird have been identified, including the white-backed vulture (1) often seen in large groups, hissing and squealing as they squabble over a carcass.

The ground squirrel **(4)** is constantly on the alert for predators, especially eagles, snakes and jackals. To protect itself from the intense Kalahari sun this rodent curls its bushy tail up over its head to form a parasol, but if the heat becomes too intense it takes refuge in the cool depths of its burrow.

The red hartebeest **(5)** was once in danger of becoming extinct because of wanton hunting, but today is plentiful in the Park. When water is available this grazing antelope will drink regularly, but in times of scarcity it seems able to go for months without drinking.

The ancient and mostly waterless 'rivers' of the Kalahari Gemsbok National Park, the Auob and, forming the eastern border with Botswana, the Nossob (which flows perhaps once every ten or so years) are the underground sources that nurture much of the reserve's prolific game population. Visitors might spot leopard (1) if they are lucky; will almost certainly see the black-backed jackal (2), springbok (4), bat-eared fox (5) and the striking gemsbok (3), which lends its name to the park. The antelope's magnificent long, sharp horns are formidable weapons of defence and are used to good effect against foes – there are accounts of even lions being bested by gemsbok.

The gemsbok also has a unique defence against another enemy – the heat. In the desert where there is little shade the danger of an animal's blood overheating and causing brain damage is ever present. The gemsbok, however, has a fine network of vessels in the nose through which blood passes *en route* to the brain. As it moves through this 'radiator' it is cooled by air inhaled through the gemsbok's nose.

4

5

Springtime in Namaqualand. One of only two true desert regions in South Africa, the wide strip of terraced sandveld leading up the west coast to the desolate lower reaches of the Orange River comes alive with a myriad wild flowers from about mid-August to mid-October each year. First to make their appearance are the white daisies (*Dimorphotheca* spp.) and *Oxalis* in all their forms and colours. Light-purple wild cineraria, darker purple *Lachenalia* and the famed red and orange Namaqualand daisies (*Ursinia* spp.) follow later.

1

2

3

4

5

At the peak of the season, mid-September under ideal conditions, the visitor is rewarded with an unforgettable sight of multi-hued carpets of blooms stretching far to the horizon (2). Close-up, the individual flowers are just as lovely: *Gazania krebsiana* (1); *Ursinia* spp. (3), the classic Namaqualand daisy; *Drosanthemum hispidum* (4), a member of the great pan-tropical mesembryanthemum family which is centred in South Africa, where over 2 000 species have been recorded; and *Cheiridopsis marlothii* (5), found in hilly places.

The Namaqualand village of Steinkopf (1) was originally established for the Nama Hottentot community. The round 'matjie and sack' houses are designed for shelter from torrid sun rather than wind and rain, which are minimal. This is copper country: the Namas worked with metal long before the white man came; settler expeditions, one led by Commander Simon van der Stel himself, set out in the 1680s in search of the seams. The mines are still active: mills at Nababiep, Carolusberg and O'Kiep each handle over 2 000 tons of ore a day.

Far to the south of Steinkopf are the towns of Nieuwoudtville where, as with so many platteland towns, the Dutch Reformed Church (**3**) is the central feature, and Calvinia (**4**), on the fringes of Namaqualand some 70 kilometres to the east. Calvinia, centre of South Africa's second largest wool-producing region after Harrismith in the Orange Free State, is an isolated little inland town set against the western edge of the Karoo and overlooked by the Hantam mountains.

The presence of spring flowers breaks the monotony of the harsh landscape (**2 & 5**) where drought is perennial and windmills tap underground water to sustain the farms.

The Cape's west coast is a region of harsh, lonely, beautiful stretches of rocky, sand-blown shorelines backed by raised beaches; of sparse and hardy vegetation, and of occasional exquisite little bays, some such as Lamberts Bay (2) and Doringbaai (3), providing safe anchorage for fishing fleets. Climate, the nature of the land and of the sea are influenced by the cold north-flowing Benguela current, which enriches the inshore Atlantic Ocean with nitrates and oxygen. Marine life thrives, sustaining both the country's fishing industry and seabirds – millions of them.

For the Cape cormorant (1) anything from scraps of vegetation to a frayed twist of nylon rope is acceptable in the making of its rude nest. Bird Island (4 & 5) is aptly named for here, as on many of the offshore islands along the West Coast, seabirds nest and roost in bewildering numbers. The gannet skypointing (6) does so to indicate non-aggressive intentions towards neighbouring birds.

4

5

6

1

2

3

The West Coast's Saldanha Bay **(2)** is one of the very few natural harbours along South Africa's entire shoreline: the first settlers, however, chose the more exposed Table Bay for its fresh water resources. Saldanha, though, is headquarters of a lively fishing and fish-processing industry, outlet for iron, manganese and other northern Cape mineral ores, and site of a naval training centre. A long narrow waterway extends southwards from Saldanha Bay, forming Langebaan Lagoon, a conservation area (now being developed as the Langebaan National Park) and playground for water sport enthusiasts **(3)**. Marcus Island **(1)** is part of the Park and home to colonies of jackass penguins, so-named for their call, which resembles the bray of a donkey. To the north of Saldanha lies a number of tiny fishing communities such as that of Paternoster **(5)** at Cape Columbine and the beautiful, unspoilt sweep of St Helena Bay **(4)**.

4

5

Inland from the southern West Coast, the landscape becomes gentler **(1)** with farmlands sprawling way into the distance – wheat, grapes and citrus are all grown on the fertile plains of the Olifants River valley. To the east of Clanwilliam in the north and Citrusdal in the south, however, the land rises abruptly into the Cedarberg. Although a few remote farms nestle in the more accessible valleys of the range and herds of

1

goats **(2)** may be seen in the higher terrain, the greater portion of the Cedarberg is a vast wilderness area some 71 000 hectares in extent. Entrance to the area is restricted, but for hikers and climbers it is well worth the minor inconvenience of obtaining a permit to spend time among the crags and peaks with their bizarre rock formations, cascading mountain streams, unique flora and magnificent views.

2

4

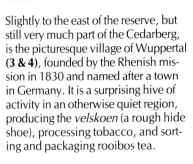

Slightly to the east of the reserve, but still very much part of the Cedarberg, is the picturesque village of Wuppertal **(3 & 4)**, founded by the Rhenish mission in 1830 and named after a town in Germany. It is a surprising hive of activity in an otherwise quiet region, producing the *velskoen* (a rough hide shoe), processing tobacco, and sorting and packaging rooibos tea.

3

The haunting world of the Cedarberg where weird, eroded rock formations (2 & 4) dominate the skyline, dwarfing the intruder. Bushmen once took refuge among these krantzes and kloofs, but the only evidence of their presence is the remains of their subtle and sensitive art (1), reminding us here that many animals, too, are long gone from the region. Among the survivors are numerous reptile species such as *Pseudocordylus capensis,* the crag lizard, (3) which continue to soak up the sun as they have for aeons past.

In his campaign against Boer guerilla commandos in the later stages of the Anglo-Boer War, Lord Kitchener erected 8 000 blockhouses such as this one **(1)** guarding a rail bridge near Wolseley. By contrast, Tulbagh **(2-5)**, set in a peaceful valley at the foot of the Witsenberg range, charms the eye and rests the spirit. Founded in 1699, it began to assume its present, dignified character in the 1790s. Part of the town was destroyed by earthquake in 1969, but restoration work has repaired much of the damage done to its historic past: in Kerk Street alone, 32 buildings, including the one shown **(4)**, have been rebuilt and now form the largest concentration of national monuments in South Africa. Among the elegant gabled houses of Tulbagh are also Cape Dutch homes with simple but no less pleasing lines **(3)**.

Some of the finest white wines in the country come from the Tulbagh valley, and at the Drostdy an old wine press stands sentinel **(2)**.

To the east of Tulbagh is the picturesque town of Ceres, embraced by grand mountains that, like the high twin peaks of Mostertshoek **(6)**, are regularly capped with snow in winter.

The south-western Cape is a land of mountains and valleys, few so spectacular as those of the Hex River area **(1)**, its scenic richness well matched by the wealth of its vineyards – the area produces most of the table grapes exported from the country.

The rolling countryside at the foot of the mountains of the southern Cape is also lush farming land **(2 & 4)** characterized by great fields of wheat. Near to the town of Swellendam, which lies in the fertile valley of the Breede River beneath the peaks of the Langeberg, is the Bontebok National Park, a haven for a now substantial bontebok population **(3)**. The species came close to extinction in the 1930s and was saved only by the timely action of a few concerned farmers who gave it sanctuary. The original park was started with a breeding stock of just 17, but poor grazing and other problems prevented success and the antelope only began to thrive when the park was transferred to its present site. Today there are more than 400. The park is also rich with other animals and birdlife is particularly prolific. Here a malachite sunbird **(5)** feeds from the common pincushion protea *Leucospermum cordifolium*.

2

3

4

5

The De Hoop Nature Reserve **(1)** near Bredasdorp is sanctuary for 1 400 plant species – most falling into the coastal fynbos classification and of which 25 are considered rare or endangered – and for a number of Cape mountain zebra **(6)**, also a threatened species. The reserve has been the centre of a major controversy between conservationists and the authorities, who, during the apartheid years, allocated part of the area for use by the military. The flower-strewn coastline east of the Cape Peninsula has wide sandy beaches, attractive embayments, small fishing communities, seaside towns and villages, as well as camps and caravan parks that draw Capetonian weekenders in their droves. Among them are Gordon's Bay **(2)**, a yachstsman's paradise tucked into the eastern corner of False Bay, Pringle Bay **(4)** near Cape Hangklip, and Hermanus **(5)**, originally a fishing village, now a substantial

residential and holiday centre, renowned within the angling fraternity. Hermanus is also internationally famed for the whales that its offshore waters host during the winter months. These are mostly gigantic southern rights, who swim into Walker Bay to calve, and whose arrival is heralded by the town's 'Whale Crier' (7). Special parties of whale-watchers fly in from around the world to witness the remarkable spectacle. Picture (3) shows a ramshackle fisherman's cottage at Waenhuiskrans (alternatively known as Arniston) near Cape Agulhas, southernmost point of the African continent.

The Cape winelands are famed not only for the wines they produce but for the exceptional beauty of their towns, villages and countryside. Stellenbosch, founded by Governor Simon van der Stel in 1679, is the oldest of the larger settlements and the second oldest town in South Africa. Age apart, however, many of its his-

torical buildings, such as Krige's Cottages (1) and oak-lined vistas such as the one leading to the Dutch Reformed Church (2), make Stellenbosch a tourist attraction in its own right. The town has great vitality, too, for it is the hub of the winelands and the seat of the University of Stellenbosch.

The gracious Lanzerac Hotel (3), just outside Stellenbosch, is famed for its lunchtime spread and a popular stop-off for visitors to the town. The homestead at 'Meerlust' (4), a prominent wine estate in the region, shows Cape Dutch architecture at its best and although it is not open to the public, many such as 'Simonsig' (5 & 6) are. These estates and other cellars are visited by hundreds of thousands of people each year, eager to see how wine is made and to sample the produce.

Franschhoek – 'French corner' in translation – takes its name from the hardy Huguenot pioneers, French refugees from the religious persecution of the 17th century's Counter-Reformation, who settled in the countryside north-east of the Cape Peninsula in 1688. Industrious, a few of them with some knowledge of wine-making, they were a welcome addition to the tiny and sometimes beleaguered communities. A Huguenot museum (2) and memorial (3) are prominent features of the town.

Franschhoek is at the head of the fertile Groot Drakenstein valley, hemmed in by the tall Drakenstein and Simonsberg mountains, and an important wine farming (1 & 4) and deciduous fruit growing area.

Paarl – the Pearl – is a lovely town of many whitewashed period buildings nestling in a broad valley (**2**) at the foot of great granite domes (**3**) which, often glistening in the sunlight, have given the town its name. The stately old Nederduits Gereformeerde Kerk (**4**) is but one of Paarl's noteworthy buildings.

Second only to Stellenbosch as a wine capital, Paarl is the headquarters of the KWV, a para-statal body which presides over the affairs of the wine industry. The KWV is also an important winery and distillery in its own right and holds tours to its cellars, where huge oaken barrels (**1**) can be seen.

Best known of the Cape's wineries is probably Nederburg (**6 & 7**), founded close to Paarl in 1792 and now producing many fine vintages of certified Superior quality. The Nederburg Auction – a heady affair of lunching, tasting, sociability and serious business – is held each autumn (**5**). It is run by Sotheby's and on offer are vintages from the country's leading cellars.

5

6

7

Close to two million people live in greater Cape Town, a city of beauty and contrast sprawling around the grandeur of Table Mountain and over the hills and shores of a Peninsula that accepted, if not welcomed, South Africa's first white settlers.

For much of the summer a strong south-easter blows across False and Table bays, gusting unnervingly through the streets of city and suburb; in winter it is wet – and windy. But when the weather is good it is perfect, and Capetonians go about their mostly gentle pursuits with a lightness of spirit that has something to do with the clarity of the air, the greenness of the hills, the history in the stones, with the fine calendar of arts and entertainment – and a lot to do with their own undemanding priorities and innate good taste.

2

1

3

4

5

Along the eastern flank of Table Mountain are: Rhodes Memorial (2) looking north across the Cape Flats, with its tea garden (1) and fallow deer (4) – the forests and footpaths round about are well trodden by the city's burgeoning jogger population (3); Groot Constantia (5), one of the earliest and certainly the most imposing of the early Cape Dutch homesteads. It began as the private residence of Simon van der Stel, the Cape's first Governor and a man of simple but refined tastes, who supervised its construction and extension with loving patience, incorporating, as one writer has put it, 'European ideas, Asian craftsmanship and African materials'. From the very first years the estate produced its own, splendid wine.

The botanic gardens at Kirstenbosch (6) where many exotic and indigenous plants are grown, including South Africa's national flower, the giant *Protea cynaroides* (7), and the University of Cape Town (8) which enjoys one of the grandest settings of any university anywhere in the world.

7

8

4

False Bay, so-named because early navigators returning from the east often mistook it for Table Bay, loops in a broad arc from Cape Point in the west to Cape Hangklip in the east. Its coastline is over 100 kilometres long, with the rapidly developing town of the Strand (5) at the base of its east-

5

6

7

ern arm. Across the bay, following the gentle sweep of white beaches interrupted by the odd rocky bluff, is Muizenberg of which Rudyard Kipling, who loved his summers at the Cape, wrote: 'White as the sands of Muizenberg, spun before the gale.' Indeed, it is only the regular blasting of summer winds that spoils the wide beach with its safe, warm surf. Nevertheless, the resort suburb, its beachfront dominated by the Pavilion (4) and other amusements, is a popular venue for beach lovers and any number of watersport competitions (6).

Continuing the coastal drive from Muizenberg one passes through the pretty fishing harbour of Kalk Bay (3) – the naval base of Simonstown can be seen across the bay – and eventually reaches the Cape Point Nature Reserve (1) at the southern tip of the Peninsula. The reserve's wildlife includes bontebok, eland, mountain zebra and baboons (2) which can prove a hazard for hikers and picnickers (visitors are urged not to feed them).

Silvermine is another of the Peninsula's reserves, and vantage points here command dramatic views over the Cape Flats and beyond to the Hottentots Holland mountains (7).

Returning from Cape Point along the western seaboard of the Peninsula the road clings tenuously to cliffs dropping sheer to the sea below. The winding route rates as one of the most spectacular scenic drives in the world and provides breathtaking views of places such as Noordhoek (1) with white sands stretching to distant Kommetjie; Hout Bay (4) with its picturesque, if sometimes noisome, fishing harbour (2); and Llandudno (3), an elite residential village surrounding a small secluded bay. Closer towards the city centre the air of tranquility changes abruptly as one reaches the built-up flatland of cosmopolitan Sea Point (6, 7 & 8) and, nearby, the famed beaches of Clifton (5).

Cape Town's old Lutheran Church (3) in Strand Street is one of the city's more dignified landmarks. It was built in 1774 as a storeroom by one Martin Melck, a devout Lutheran tradesman determined to circumvent a prohibition on places of worship other than Dutch Reformed.

Long Street was, until quite recently, the vibrant scene of the seamier kind of sociability. Now quieter, with much of its earlier architecture gone, there is still a hint of its past in one of the few remaining Victorian façades (1).

The South African Cultural Museum (2) adjoining the Gardens at the head of Adderley Street was the Old Supreme Court which was restored in the 1960s to house a number of important collections. The original building on the site was the slave lodge of the Dutch East India Company.

The Herbert Baker-designed Houses of Parliament (4) also number among the many splendid buildings that grace the bounds of Cape Town's Gardens — charming heir to Van Riebeeck's prosaic vegetable patch and internation-

ally famed for the wealth of its exotic trees, shrubs and flowers. Feeding the grey squirrels in the Gardens is a favourite pastime for youngsters (5); these engaging little animals are not indigenous to the country — they were introduced by Cecil John Rhodes. The Gardens Synagogue (8) is flanked by handsome oaks, some dating back to the time of the Cape's first Governor.

Once waves broke at the massive ramparts of the five-bastioned Castle of Good Hope (6) built between 1666 and 1679. Extensive reclamation has since pushed the ocean far back and the crash of surf has given way to the rumble of trains.

The Malay Quarter, or *Bokaap*, (7), where many of the city's Moslems live, is a dense huddle of cottages, some of them charmingly restored.

Cape Town's City Hall **(1)** has been replaced as the capital's administrative centre by the new Civic Centre, but not in the affections of Capetonians: some fine symphony concerts are performed in its massively-chandeliered auditorium. The grand Edwardian building overlooks the Grand Parade **(2, 3 & 4)**, mid-week and Saturday meeting place where anything from a bunch of freshly cut flowers to a bolt of material can be purchased.

Open air markets are very much part of the city's street scene, and much favoured among locals and visitors alike is the one in cobble-stoned Greenmarket Square **(5 & 7)**.

Cape Town's streets belong to the people and even in Adderley Street **(8)**, the city's main thoroughfare, pedestrians rule the roads, paying scant attention to motor vehicles and traffic lights. Adderley Street, too, is a place for parades – everything from the sedate opening of Parliament cavalcade to the varsity rag procession. Here **(6)** are participants in the annual Cape Town Festival. The street, once part of the grand Heerengracht thoroughfare, was named after Charles Adderley, a 19th century British politician who fought hard and successfully to prevent the settlement of convicts at the Cape.

During the apartheid era Robben Island, just off Table Bay, served as a maximum security prison, its most famous inmate Nelson Mandela, now President of South Africa. Its history, though, goes much further back, to the beginnings of white settlement; among its historic structures is the attractive lighthouse **(1)** and Anglican church **(2)**, designed by the renowned turn-of-the-century architect Herbert Baker. The island is likely to feature prominently in Cape Town's tourism plans; there are proposals for developing a nature and marine reserve, and for preserving the prison as a museum – and as a memorial to victims of political injustice. Cape Town huddles between Table Mountain and Table Bay **(3, 4** and **7)**, and until about 50 years ago city and harbour were intimately connected. But with land reclamation and motorway construction, the links were broken. Now they are being restored – by the hugely ambitious and imaginative Victoria and Alfed Waterfront development **(5)**, a fantasia of historic buildings (many renovated and adapted for new purposes), museums, marinas, charming apartment blocks, open quaysides, promenades, public squares, walkways and waterways, markets, glittering malls **(6)**, speciality shops, theatres, cinemas, restaurants, bistros and pubs.

1

2

3

4

Over a thousand metres high, monolithic, misty, moody, ever-changing with wind and season, Table Mountain (**5**) dominates the horizon, captivates the Capetonian heart. The mountain offers breathtaking views of city and sea from its summit, reached either by walking (**3**) (some paths are undemanding, others are extremely strenuous), climbing or by cable car (**1**).

Table Mountain has been proclaimed a National Monument and a sanctuary for its, in some cases unique, flora and fauna. Among the thousands of species are *Psoralea pinnata* (**2**); *Leucospermum cordifolium* (a member of the protea family) with a Cape sugarbird perched on its flowerhead (**4**); *Polygala bracteolata* (**6**); and *Helipterim speciosissimum* (**7**).

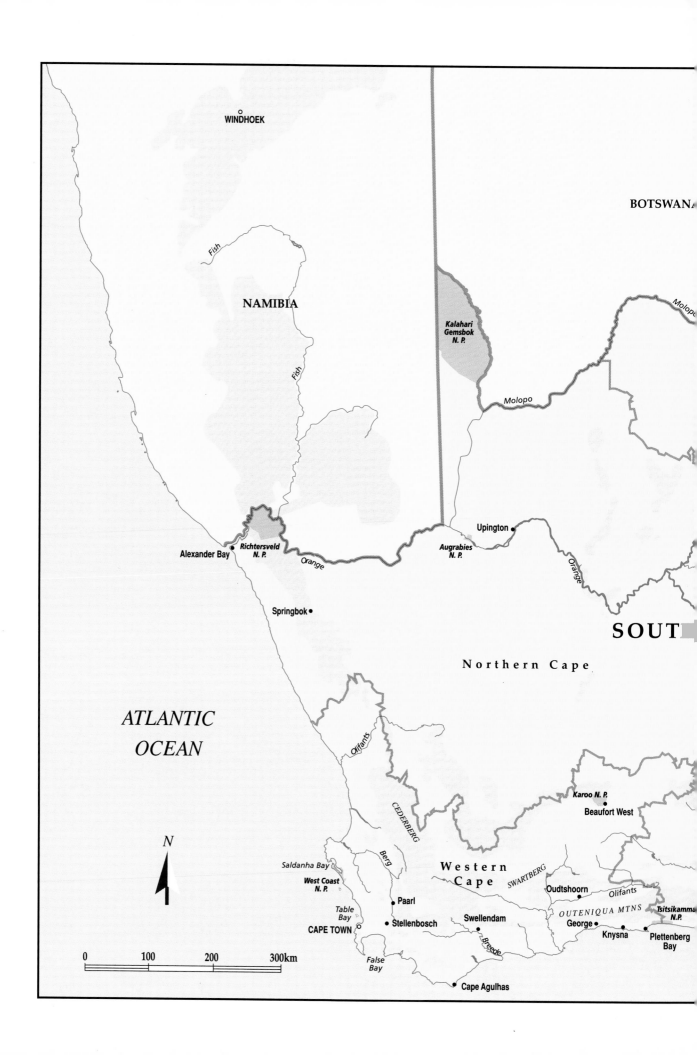

INDEX

Page numbers listed in **bold** typeface indicate illustrated references.

Abyssinia 29
Act of Union 21, 28, 41
Adderley Street 21, **23**
Addo Elephant National Park 48, **139**
administrative capital 14, 15
African National Congress (ANC) 12, 14, 32, 33, 34, 35, 38, 39, 40, **43**, 45
Afrikaans language 12, 33
Afrikaner community 12, 13, 25
    identity 27
    power 29
    settlement 26
Afrikanerdom 32
agriculture, farming 13, 14, 39, 41, 45
    fruits, canned 45
    fruits, fresh-frozen 45
    meat 45
    sugar plantations 12, 45, **108**
    wine 20, 45, **184-190**
    wool 45
Agriculture Credit Board 45
Agulhas, Cape 7, 18
Agulhas Current 7, 10
Alberton 15
Algoa Bay 13, 19, 24, 138
Amersfoort 21
Amsterdam 20
anglicization policies 28
Anglo-Boer War **17, 22**, 25, 33
Anglo-Dutch wars 21
Angola 33, 40
Angolan civil war 35
Angoni 25
Antwerp 19
apartheid 10, 29, **30**, 35, **37**, 38, 46
Apla 40
Appellate Division of the Supreme Court 32, 41
Armscor 40
arts, the 46
Asian people 12
    settlement 27
Asiatic Land Tenure Act 12
Atlantic Ocean 7, 19
Augrabies Falls National Park 48, **160-161**
Autshumao, Harry 20

Baker, Herbert 15
Bantu-speaking people 18, 24
Barlow, Eddie 47
Barnato, Barney 27
Basutoland (Lesotho) 26, 28
Batavia 19, 20
Bathurst 25
Baxter Theatre (Cape Town) 46
Beagle 15
Bechuanaland (Botswana) 26, 27, 28
Bedfordview 15
Benguela Current 7, 10
Benoni 15
Berg River 6
Berg River Valley 21
Big Hole (Kimberley) **16**, 27, 158, **159**
Biko, Steve 34
Bill of Rights 39, 40
Bisho 14
Black Authorities Act 32
black
    consciousness organizations 33, 34, 35
    customs and traditions 11
    education 33
    labour 32, 34
    people, dissension 25
    property ownership 34
    settlement 27
    trade unions 34
    urbanization 32
    violence 33
    armed struggle 38
    discrimination 32, 34
    struggle 19
Black Flag Rebellion 27

Black Sash **30**
Bloemfontein 14, 15, 41, **92-93**
Bloemfontein Convention 26
Bloemfontein Opera House 15
Blood River 25
Bloukrans River 25
Blue Train 45
Bluff (Durban) 7
Boers 19, 24
    concentration camps **17**, 28
    dissension 25
    settlement 27
    the Great Trek 24
Boesak, the Reverend Allan **42**
Boipatong 38
Bokaap (Cape Malay Quarters) **197**
Boksburg 15, 44
Boland 45
Bontebok National Park 48, 180, **181**
Boom, Annetje 20
Boomplaats, Battle of 26
Bophuthatswana (North West) 14, **64-65**
Boschheuvel (Bishopscourt) 20
Botha, General Louis 13, **17**, 27, 28
Botha, President P.W. **23**, 34, 35, 44
Botswana 33, 34, 162
boycott, cultural 46
Brand, Jan 26
Brazzaville (Congo Republic) 35
Brazzaville Protocol 35
Brink, André 47
British administrators 24
    annexation **16**, 26, 27
    colonial administration 24
    occupation of the Cape 13, 26
    people 19
    royal visit **8-9, 30**
    rule 13
    settlement **8, 9**, 15, 26, 27
    dissension 25
British Black Week 27
British Liberal Ministers 28
British Occupation, First 26
Buchan, John (Lord Tweedsmuir) 28
Buffalo River 7
Buller, Captain 24
Buller, Sir Redvers 27
Bushman paintings 18, **102**, 103, 150, **155**
Bushman (San) people 18, 24
Bushmans River 24, 25, 100, **101**
business community, white 11
Buthelezi, Chief Mangosuthu 11, 34, 38, **43**
bywoners (tenant farmers) 29

Cahora Bassa Dam 40
Cairo 35
Caledon River 6
Campbell, Roy 47
Cape Colony 27
Cape Dutch architecture 20, 21, **184-185**
Cape Flats 12
Cape Fold mountains 6
Cape Malays (Muslims) 12
Cape of Good Hope 21
Cape Peninsula 7, 10, 14, **190-195**
Cape Point 7, 18
Cape Point Nature Reserve **193**, 194
Cape Province 14, **134-139, 140-147, 158-175**
Cape Provincial Council 28
Cape Town 7, 10, 14, 21, 24, 32, 44, 47, **196-201**
Cape-Dutch Settlers 12
Carnarvon, Lord 26
Carnegie Corporation 29
Carter Administration 33
Castle of Good Hope, the 20, 24, **197**
Cederberg 6, 21, **174-177**
Cetshwayo (Zulu king) 26
Chamberlain, Joseph 27
Charter of Fundamental Rights 39
Charter of Justice 41

chemicals and pharmaceuticals 44
children's courts 41
Chinese people 12
    labour 28
Christian faith 12
Church Square (Pretoria) 15
Churchill, Sir Winston **23**, 29
circuit courts 41
Ciskei 11, 14, 38
Civil Co-operation Bureau (CCB) 35
Clifton 7
climate 7
clinics 46
clothing and textiles 45
Coetsee, Jacobus 21
Coetzee, J.M. 47
Colenso 27
colonial power 29
coloured (mixed-descent)
    communities 12
    laws 32
Coloured Persons Representative Council (CRC) 32
'coloured vote' 28
commerce 41
commissioners court 41
Commonwealth 32
Commonwealth of Nations 29, 39
Comprehensive Anti-Apartheid Act 38
Concerned South Africans Group (Cosag) 38
Congo Republic, The 40
Congress Alliance 33
Congress of Democrats 33
Congress of South African Trade Unions (Cosatu) 45
conscription 40
conservation 39
Constantia 13
Constitutional Court 39, 41
constitutional dispensation 34
constitution, the 39
consumer boycott 12
Convention for a Democratic South Africa (Codesa) 38, 43
Convention of Pretoria 26
Corpus Juris Civilis 41
cost of living 46
Criminal Law Amendment Bill 33
Cruse, Hieronimus 21
Cuban withdrawal 35
cultural affairs 39
Curtis, Lionel 28
Customs Union 40
Cuyler, Colonel Jacob 24

Da Nova, João 19
dairy products 45
Danckaert, Jan 21
Davenport, T.R.H. 32
Dawson, Geoffrey 28
De Beers 27
De Choisy, Abbé 21
De Houtman (brothers) 19
De Klerk, President F.W. 35, 38, 39, **42**
De Wet, Christiaan **17**, 27, 29
decentralization 10
defence 40
Delagoa Bay (Maputo) 25
Delville Wood 29
democratic election 35, 38, **43**
Department of Information 34
deserts and semi-deserts 6
'destabilization' policy 33
Dias, Bartholomeu 18
Diego Cão 19
Difaqane 25
Dingaan (Zulu king) 25
'dirty tricks' campaign 38
disease 20, 28
district health authorities 46
District Six 12
Donald, Allan 47
Drake, Sir Francis 18

Drakensberg 25
    Natal 5, 6, 14, **96-103**
    Transvaal 5, 14, **70-71**
Drakenstein mountains 6
Drommedaris 20
Duncan, Governor-General Patrick 28
Dunrobin Castle 7
Durban 7, 15, 24, 25, 26, 33, **112-119**
Durban University 13
Durban-Pinetown complex 10, 12, 15
Dutch East India Company 13, 19, 20, 21
Dutch language 28
    settlers 12
dwarf bush vegetation 7

East Coast 7
East London 7, 14, 26, **134-135**
eastern Cape 13, 18, 24, 32
Eastern Cape province 10, 11, 14
Eastern Transvaal 6, 10, 14, 44, 45
eco-tourism 47
economic balance 11
    development 40
    recession 10, 35
economy 41
Edenvale 15
Edict of Nantes 20
education 46
Egypt 18
elections
    democratic 38, **43**
    general (1987) 35
    general (1989) 35
    general (1994) 38, **43**
    parliamentary election (1910) 28
    self-governing colonies 28
electricity 40, 41, 44
Electricity Supply Commission (Eskom) 40, 44
Els, Ernie 47
Embumbula 15
employment 46
English language 13, 28
English-speaking community 27
Erasmus Commission 34
Ethiopia 40
ethnic groups 10, 11
Europe 29
European people 12, 13, 18
European Western Front 29
European [Economic] Community 38
executive authority, the 39

False Bay 7, **182-183**, 190, **192-193**
Farewell, Lieutenant Francis **9**, 15, 24
fishing industry **170, 172-173**
Ferreira, Wayne 47
Festival of the Arts, Grahamstown 46
Fordyce, Bruce 47
foreign debt 44
    policy 39
forestry 45
Franschhoek 20, **186-187**
'free-burghers' 20, 21
Freedom Alliance 38
Freedom Charter 12, 33
French revolution 13
Frontier Wars **9**, 24
Fugard, Athol 47
fynbos 6

Gabbema, Abraham 21
gambling 39
game parks and nature reserves 46-48, **67, 76-89, 94-97, 100-103, 120-129, 141, 157, 161-165, 175, 182, 192-193**
game products 45
Gamka River Valley (The Hell) 151
Gamtoos River 21
Gandhi, Mohandas K. (Mahatma) 12, **22**, 29, 33
Garden Route 7, 48, **140-147**
Gardens 21

Gardens Synagogue **197**
Gardiner, Allen 24
GATT agreement 45
General Law Amendment Act (Sabotage Act) 34
George **147**
Germiston 15
Giant's Castle 48
Goede Hoop 20
Goldberg, Dennis 34
Golden Gate Highlands National Park 48, **94-95**
Gold Reef City **52-53**
Goldstone commission 38
Gordimer, Nadine 47
Gordon's Bay **182**
government of national unity 11
Graaff, Sir De Villiers **30**
Graaff-Reinet 5, 21, **155**
Grahamstown 15, 24, **136**
Grand Parade 24
Great Brak River 21
Great Depression 29
Great Fish River 6, 21, 24
Great Karoo 6, 14, 48
Great Trek 24, 25
Greater Windhoek mountains 6
Griquas 12, 18
Griqualand West 27
Groot Constantia **190**
Groot Vloer 6
Gross Domestic Product 41, 44
Group Areas Act 32, 35

Hani, Chris 38, 43
Harms commission of enquiry 35
Hartzenberg, Ferdinand 34
health and health care 39, 40, 46
Heerengracht 21
Hendrik Verwoerd Dam 6
Hendrickse, the Reverend Allen **37**
Hermanus **183**
Herodotus 18
Herold's Bay **146-147**
Hertzog, J.B.M. (Barry) 13, 27, **23**, 29
Het Volk (Afrikaner organization) 28
Hex River Valley **180**
High Commission territories 28
Hluhluwe Game Reserve 48
Holland 19
homelands (national states) 14, 32, 38
Hopetown **156**
hospitals 46
Hottentot people 12
Hottentots Holland mountain range 6, 20, **193**
Houses of Parliament 32, **197**
housing 39, 46
Howick Falls **109**
Huguenots, French **8**, 13
Huguenot memorial **187**
Human Rights Commission 38
Humansdorp **139**

Immorality Act 35
Imperial Army 29
Imperial power 26
Imperial War Cabinet 29
impis (Zulu warriors) 25
India 32
Indian Ocean 7, 14, 19
Indian people **9**, 12, 15, **51**, **110**, **118**
industrial expansion 10
industrialization 41
industry 40, 44
influx control 10, 34
informal sector, the 46
Information Scandal 34
Inkatha Freedom Party (IFP) 14, 38, **43**
ISCOR (South African Iron and Steel Corporation) 29
Islamic traditions 12
Italy 29
Itinerario 19
Ivory Coast 33

Jabavu, John Tengo 33
Jameson Raid 13, 27

Jameson, Dr Leander Starr 15, 27
Janszen, Leendert 19
Jewish community 13
Johannesburg 14, 15, 27, 33, **49-55**
Johannesburg Stock Exchange 44
judicial capital 14, 15
Judicial Services Commission 39

Kalahari 6, 14, 18
Kalahari Gemsbok National Park 48, **162-163**
Kamiesberg 5
KaNgwane 11
Karoo 5, 14, **152-153**
Karoo National Park 48, **152-153**
Kasis, Professor T. 33
Kaunda, Kenneth 33
Kei River 21, 24
Kempton Park 15
Kente, Gibson 47
Kenya 40
Kerr, Philip 28
Khoikhoi (Hottentots) 18, 19, 20, 21, 24, 25
Kimberley 10, 13, 14, 27, 28, **158-159**
Kings Beach (Port Elizabeth) **139**
King William's Town 14, 26, **135**
Kirkwood 15
Kirstenbosch **191**
Kissinger, Henry 33
Kitchener, General Horatio **17**, 27
Klerksdorp 14
Kliptown 33
Knysna 48, **144-145**
Koopmans de Wet House 24
Korana people 18
Kruger National Park 6, 14, 47, 48, **76-89**
Kruger, Paul **16**, 26, 27
Krugersdorp 15
Kunene River 40
KwaZulu 38, **104-107**
KwaZulu-Natal 7, 10, 13, 14, 18, 38, 45

Labour 45
Indian 26
Labour Party 34
Ladysmith 27
Laingsburg **153**
Lake Malawi 25, 40
Lake Victoria 40
Lamberts Bay **170**
Land Bank 45
landdrost (magistrate) 21, 24
Langebaan lagoon 48
Langeberg 6
Later Iron Age 18
League of Nations 29
legal system 41
legislative capital 14, 15
Leroux, Etienne 47
Lesotho 33, 34
Lesotho Highlands Water Scheme 6
Letaba River 6, **89**
Liberia 33
Libya 18, 40
Liesbeeck River 21
Limpopo River 6, 14, 18, 25
liquid and gas fuels 44
Lisbon 19
Little Karoo 6
local government 39
Lords Seventeen, The 19
Lost City **64-65**
Lowveld 6
Luanda 40
Lubowski, Anton 35
Lüderitz Bay 29
Luthuli, Chief Albert **31**, 33
Luvuvhu River **78**

Macmillan, Harold 32
Mafeking 27
Magaliesberg 14
Magersfontein 27
magisterial districts 14, 21
magistrates 41
Magoebaskloof **69**

mail ships **31**
maintenance courts 41
maize 40, 45
Majuba Hill **17**, 26
Malabar 19
Malan, Dr D.F. 13, 29, **30**, 32
Malan, François 28
Malan, Magnus 35
Malawi 33
Malmesbury 21
Maluti Mountains **91**
Mandela, President Nelson 33, 34, 35, 38, 40, **42-43**, 46
Mandela, Winnie **42**
manufacturing industry 41
Marais, Eugène 47
Market Theatre, Johannesburg 46
Matabele empire 25
Mbeki, Thabo 39
Merriman, Premier J.X. 28
metal industries 44
metals and minerals 5
Meyer, Elana 47
Middelburg 14
military vehicles 40
weapons 40
Milner, Lord Alfred **22**, 27, 28
Milnerton 7
minerals 40
mining 13, 14, 41, 44
andalusite 44
asbestos 44
chrome 5
chromium 44
coal 5, 44
cobalt 5
coke 44
copper 5
diamonds 13, 14, 27, 44, **158-159**
fluorspar 44
gold 5, 13, 15, 44, 27, 28, 29, **58-59**, 72
iridium 44
iron-ore 44
manganese 44
nickel 5, 44
palladium 44
phosphates 44
platinum 5, 44
rhodium 44
ruthenium 44
steel 40
tar 44
uranium 5, 44
vanadium 44
zinc 5
Minister of Justice 41
Mitchell, Brian 47
Mitchell's Plain 12
Mixed Marriages Act 34, 35
Mkuzi Game Reserve 48, **124-127**
Mmabatho 14
Molucca Islands 18
Mossel Bay 7, 19, 21, 44
Mostertshoek **179**
Mountain Zebra National Park 48, **155**
Mozambique 11, 19, 25, 34, 35
Muizenberg 21
Mulder, Dr Connie 34
multi-national development 32
Mussolini, Benito 29
Mzilikazi (Ndebele leader) 11, 25, 26

Nama people 18, **168**
Namaqualand 5, 6, 10, 14, 21, **166-169**
Namib Desert 10
Namibia 5, 18, 19, 29, 35
Namibian independence 33, 35
Napoleonic wars 13
Natal 12, 13, 15, 24, 25, 26, 28, 32, **96-103**, **108-131**
Natal Indian Congress 12, 33
Natal Native Congress 33
Natalia, Boer Republic of 25
National Assembly 38, 39
national budget 41
National Convention **22**, 28
National Party 14, 29, 32, 34, 35

National Peacekeeping Force 40
National Security Management System 35
Native (Urban Areas) Act 32
Native Affairs Commission 28
Naude, Dr Beyers **42**
Ndumi Game Reserve 10, 48, **128-129**
Nelspruit 14
Netherlands 19
Newlands 7
Nguni-speaking people 10, 18, 26
Ngwane clan 25
Nico Malan Theatre, Cape Town 46
Nieuw Haerlem 19
Nkomati Accord 34
Nobel Peace Prize 33, 38
non-metallic mineral products 44
North West province 5, 14
northern Cape 13, 14
Northern Cape province 10, 14, 44
Northern Transvaal 14, 18, 44
Ntujuma 15

Oil 44
Old Supreme Court 21
Olifants River 6, 21, 25
Oorlam people 18
Oppenheimer, Harry 13
Oppenheimer, Sir Ernest 13, **30**
Orange Free State 5, 10, 14, 15, 26, **90-95**
Orange River 6, 7, 10, 21, 25, 26, 29, 158
Orange River Colony system 28
Orange River Scheme 6
Orange River Sovereignty 26
Orange River Valley 6
Oranje Unie (Afrikaner party) 28
Organisation of African Unity (OAU) 39, 40
Oribi Gorge **130**
Ossewabrandwag 29
Oudtshoorn **148**
Outeniqua mountains 6, 7, **148**

P.K. Le Roux Dam 6
Paarl 20, 21, 35, **188-189**
Palace of Justice 15
Pan-Africanist Congress (PAC) 32, 33, 35, 38, 40
Parliament 26
pass laws 32, 33, 34, **36**, 41
passive resistance campaigns 12
Paton, Alan **31**, 47
Peace of Vereeniging 28
petroleum 44
Pietermaritzburg 13, 14, 15, **110**
Pietermaritzburg University 13
Pietersburg 14
Pilgrim's Rest **72**
Pillars of Hercules 18
Player, Gary 47
Plettenberg Bay 14, **142-143**
police 39
political prisoners, release of 35
Pollock, Graham and Peter 47
Pondoland 26
'poor white' problem 29
population censuses 10
growth 10
Population Registration Act 35
Poqo (underground movement) 33
Port Elizabeth 10, 14, 15, 19, 44, **138-139**
Port Natal 21, 24
Portugal 18
Portuguese **8**, 19
Potgieter, Andries 25
Pretoria 7, 12, 15, 27, 33, **60-63**
Pretorius, Marthinus 26
processed foods 45
Proctor, Mike 47
produce 45
Progressive Federal Party 34
Promotion of Black Self-Government Act 32
proteas 6
protest marches 32

provincial parliament 5, 39
Provincial regions 14
Public Protector 41
PWV region 10, 14

Raadsaal 15
railways 45
Rand, commercial 35, 40, 44
    financial 44
Randburg 15
Randfontein 15
Ramaphosa, Cyril **43**
recession 15
Reconstruction and Development
    Programme (RDP) 41, 44, 45, 46
'Red Revolt' **23**, 29
Red Sea 18
referendum (1908) 28
    (1983) 34
    (1992), whites-only 38
Reform Committee 27
regional governments 38, 39
    magistrate's courts 41
    planning and development 39
    statistics 14
Reijger 20
Reitz, Deneys 27
Retief, Piet 25
Rhodes University 13, 15, **136**
Rhodes, Cecil John **16**, 27
Rhodesia 13
Rhodesian independence 33
Richards Bay 44
Richards, Barry 47
Richtersveld National Park 48
Riekert commission of enquiry 34, 45
riots 33
Rivonia Trial 34
roads 45
Robben Island 34, 43, **200**
Roberts, Lord 27
Roggeveld Scarp (Escarpment) 5
Rondebosch 20, 21
Roodepoort 15
Rorke's Drift 26
Royal Natal National Park 48, **96-97**
Rubicon speech 44
Rustenburg 14
Rwanda 40

Saldanha Bay 7, 19, **172-173**
sanctions 35, **37**, 38
Sand du Plessis Opera House
    (Bloemfontein) 46
Sand River Convention 26
Sandton 15, **52**
Sani Pass 5, **102**
São Bras 19
Sasol 44, **92**
satyagraha (passive resistance) 33
schooling 39
    languages 28
Schreiner, Olive 47
Schreiner, W.P. 28
Sea Point 7
sea-route to India 18
security 35
'securocrats' 35
Selborne Memorandum 28
Seme, Dr Pixley 33
Senate 39
Separate Amenities Act 35
separate development 32
Separate Registration of Voters Act 32
settlers 21
    Belgian 20
    British 15
    Dutch 20
    French 20

Settlers
    German 20
    Scandanavian 20
    Xhosa 21
Settlers' Monument, 1820 British 15, **136**
Shaka (Zulu king) 11, 15, 24, 25
Sharpeville **31**, 32, 33
shebeens 46
Shepstone, Sir Theophilus 26
Sisulu, Walter 34, **42**
Slabbert, Dr F. van Zyl 34
slavery 21, 24
    abolition of 25
Slovo, Joe 33
Smith, Governor Sir Harry 26
Smith, Ian 33, **36**
Smuts, General Jan 13, **23**, 27, 28,
    29, 33
Sneeuberg 5
social democracy 10
    welfare 46
Sodwana Bay **120-121**
Soekor 44
Soga, Tiyo 33
Somalia 40
Somerset, Governor Lord Charles **9**, 24
Soshangane (Zulu commander) 25
Sotho people 18, **66-67**, 91
South African Airways 45
South African Brigade 29
South African Coloured People's
    Organisation 33
South African Communist Party
    (SACP) 33, 35, **42**
South African Defence Force 40
South African Indian Congress 12
South African Iron and Steel Corporation
    (ISCOR) 29
South African National Defence Force 40
South African Native National
    Congress 33
South African Police Services 41
South Coast 7
South West Africa 5, **23**, 29
South West African People's Organisation
    (Swapo) 40
Southern African Development
    Community 40
Soutpansberg 5, 14, 25, **66**
Soweto 10, 15, 33, **36**, **56-57**
Spice Islands 19
sport and recreation 39, 46, 47, **110**, **119**
    African music 47
    athletics 47
    cricket 47
    football 47
    golf 47
    music 46, 47
    olympic games 38, 47
    radio 47
    rugby 47
    Springboks 47
    television 47
    tennis 47
Springs 15
state of emergency 34
State Theatre, Pretoria 46
Stavenisse 21
Stellenbosch 20, **184-185**
St Lucia 48, **120-121**
Stormberg 5, 27
Storms River 7
Strand Street 24
strandlopers (beachrangers) 20
Strijdom, J.G. 32
strike action 29, 32
Sudan 40
Sudwala Caves **74**
Sun City 14, **64**

Sundays River 6
Suppression of Communism Act 34
Supreme Court 41
Suurberg 5
Suzman, Helen 13
Swakopmund 19, 29
Swartberg 6
Swartvlei **145-146**
Swaziland 11, 28, 33, 34
Swellendam 21

Table Bay 7, 19, 20, 21
Table Mountain 7, 14, 18, 21, **200-203**
Tagus River 18
Tanzania 40
Temane, Matthews 47
Terre'Blanche, Eugene 38, **42**
textiles 45
Thaba Nchu 25
Thambo, Oliver 38
'third force' 35, 38
tobacco 45
Torch Commando **30**
'Total Strategy' 35
tourism 39
townships 46, 47
trade union 12, 45
traditional authorities 39
Transitional Executive Council (TEC) 38
transitional government 38
Transkei 11, 14, **131-133**
Transnet 40, 45
transport 39
    and communications 41, 45
    and equipment 44
Transvaal **70-89**
Transvaal Congress 33
Transvaal Indian Congress 12
Transvaal Indigency Commission 29
Treurnicht, Dr Andries 34
Tricameral constitutional system 34, **37**
Trichardt, Louis 25
Tsitsikamma State Forest 7, 48
Tsitsikamma mountains 6
Tsitsikamma National Park 48, **141**
Tsonga people 18
Tswana people 25
Tugela River 6, 11, 25, **96**
Tulbagh **178**
Tutu, Archbishop Desmond **42**
Tuynhuis (Government House) 21

Uitenhage 14, 15, 24
uitlanders (foreigners) 13, **16**, 27
Ulundi 14, 26
Umfolozi Game Reserve 48, **122-123**,
    125
Umkonto we Sizwe (spear of the
    nation) 33
unification of South Africa 27
Union Buildings 15, **61**
Union of South Africa 14, 15, **22**, 25,
    29, 32, 33
United Democratic Front 34
United Nations 29, 33, 39
United Party 29
United States Congress 38
universities 13, **53**, **60**, **136**, **191**
University of Cape Town (UCT) 13, **191**
University of South Africa (Unisa) **60**
University of the Witwatersrand
    (Wits) 13, **53**
Unlawful Organisations Act 33
urban drift 10
urbanization 47

Vaal Basin 6
Vaal River 6, 25, 26, 29
Vaalbos National Park 48

Valley of a Thousand Hills 109, **110-111**
Valley of Desolation 6, **154**
Value Added Tax 46
Van der Post, Laurens 47
Van der Stel, Willem Adriaan 21
Van der Stel, Simon 20, 21
Van Linschoten, Jan 19
Van Riebeeck, Jan **8**, 19, 20, 21
Vasco da Gama 19
Vegkop, Battle of **9**, 26
Venda 18, **66**
Vereeniging **17**, 28, 32
Verwoerd, Hendrik 13, **31**, 32, **36**
Vet River 25
Victor Verster prison 35
Victoria, Queen 26
Victoria Falls 6, 33, 45
Vigilance Association 33
violence, **37**, 41
    political 38
    reactionary 35
viticulture 20
Volkstaat (peoples' republic) 13, 38
Von Lettow-Vorbeck, Paul Emil 29
Voortrekkers 26, **62**
Vorster, B.J. 33, 34, **36**

Wagenaer, Commander Zacharias 20
Water schemes, pans and lakes 6
Waterberg 5, 14
Waterfront, Victoria and Alfred **201**
Webster, David 35
welfare 39
Wessels, Kepler 47
West Coast 7
West Coast National Park 48
Western Cape 10, 12, 14, 45
Western Desert 29
western Transvaal 14
Westminster, Statute of 29
Westminster system 26, 28, 34
Westonaria 15
white labour 32
    people 12
    political dominance 12, 35
    settlement 26, 27
Wiehahn commission of enquiry 34, 45
Wild Coast **131-133**
Wilderness 48
Winburg 26
Wintervogel, Jan 21
Witbank 14
Witwatersrand 12, 13, 15, 27, 28, 29
Woodstock 21
World Cup 47
World War, First 29
World War, Second 29
Wynberg 21

Xhosa people 12, 18, 24, **132**
    settlement 27
    land struggle 25

Young, Andrew 33

Zaïre 40
Zaïre (Congo) River 40
Zambezi River 6, 40
Zambia 33
Zanzibar 18
Zimbabwe 13, 25, 34, 45
Zulu people 26, **103-107**, **115**
    settlement 27
    conflict 26
'Zulu factor' 38
Zululand 25, 26, **121-129**
Zuurberg National Park 48
Zwangendaba 25
Zwelethini, King Goodwill 11